THIS IS ME! 2022

RHYMES FROM THE UK

Edited By Jenni Harrison

First published in Great Britain in 2022 by:

Young Writers
Remus House
Coltsfoot Drive
Peterborough
PE2 9BF
Telephone: 01733 890066
Website: www.youngwriters.co.uk

All Rights Reserved
Book Design by Ashley Janson
© Copyright Contributors 2022
Softback ISBN 978-1-80015-976-1

Printed and bound in the UK by BookPrintingUK
Website: www.bookprintinguk.com
YB0504R

FOREWORD

For Young Writers' latest competition This Is Me, we asked primary school pupils to look inside themselves, to think about what makes them unique, and then write a poem about it! They rose to the challenge magnificently and the result is this fantastic collection of poems in a variety of poetic styles.

Here at Young Writers our aim is to encourage creativity in children and to inspire a love of the written word, so it's great to get such an amazing response, with some absolutely fantastic poems. It's important for children to focus on and celebrate themselves and this competition allowed them to write freely and honestly, celebrating what makes them great, expressing their hopes and fears, or simply writing about their favourite things. This Is Me gave them the power of words. The result is a collection of inspirational and moving poems that also showcase their creativity and writing ability.

I'd like to congratulate all the young poets in this anthology, I hope this inspires them to continue with their creative writing.

CONTENTS

Independent Entries

Jessica Emberson — 1

Chantry Middle School, Morpeth

Florence Hall (10) — 2
Alice Leja (11) — 4
Evangeline (Evie) Ellery (10) — 5
Lilly-Mae Wall (10) — 6
Ben Young (11) — 7
Heidi Beale (10) — 8
Lillie Barton (10) — 9
Luke Smith (10) — 10
Ryan Humble (10) — 11
Eleanor Hodgson (11) — 12
Nadia Rojek (11) — 13
Alfie Egan (11) — 14

Coaltown Of Balgonie Primary School, Coaltown Of Balgonie

Lucy Methven (11) — 15
Alex Morrison (11) — 16
Emma McGibbon (11) — 18
Archie Lawson (11) — 19
Kimberley Galloway (10) — 20
Lana Summers (11) — 21
Aiden Melville (11) — 22
Daniel Proctor (11) — 23
Harry Good (10) — 24
Nicky Skinner (10) — 25
Lexi Smith (11) — 26
Abbie McLaughlin (10) — 27
Otis Leitch (11) — 28
Tianna Coppola (10) — 29

Nicol Thomson (10) — 30
Remi West (10) — 31
Connor McLean (11) — 32
Campbell Jones (11) — 33
Cameron Melville (10) — 34
Stephen Wright (11) — 35
Brooke Jones (11) — 36
Olly Webster (11) — 37

Craig Yr Hesg Primary School, Glyncoch

Ffion Cross (10) — 38
Olivia Stevens (10) — 39
Summer Griffiths (10) — 40
Olivia Carter (9) — 41
Jacob Williams (10) — 42
Mason Davies (11) — 43
Amelia Roberts (10) — 44
Callum Bowns (10) — 45
Lily May Hayman (10) — 46
Olivia Stanton (9) — 47
Skye Baker (11) — 48
Zuzanna Bachula (11) — 49
Isobel Mardon-Hughes (10) — 50
Ting Yan Harry Liu (9) — 51
Summer Green (10) — 52
Liam Richards (10) — 53
Niamh Murphy (10) — 54
Olliver McGlennon (10) — 55
Grace Morgan (9) — 56
Phyllisity Hawkins (11) — 57
Thomas Griffiths (10) — 58

Gardners Lane Primary School, Cheltenham

Raafi Hasan (9)	59
Adrin Murshed (9)	60
Ahsan Uddin (9)	61
James Holloway (10)	62
Miley Hornby (11)	63
Melany Del Cid Aguirre (10)	64
Tyler Finn (10)	65
Riyad Shalahin (9)	66
Libby Lewis-Hall (11)	67
Kiana Aswat (10)	68
Skye Clarke (11)	69
Ana Maria (9)	70
Carson (10)	71
Oscar Lightstone (10)	72
Daizzy Njoku (11)	73
Ifra Rahman (11)	74
Maisie Hester (10)	75
Oliwia Czajkowska (10)	76
Jedidiah Adedipe (10)	77
Paige Jackson (10)	78
Scarlett-Mai James (9)	79
Archie Orpin (10)	80
Evie Davis (10)	81
Srinika Pesaladinne (10)	82
Ayo	83
Sayu Sasikumar (11)	84
Archie Locke (9)	85

Mears Ashby CE Primary School, Mears Ashby

Max Perett-King (11)	86
Olivia Preston (10)	87
Brooke Browne (11)	88
Jess Cooling (10)	89
Sophia Sargent (9)	90
Elijah Borbor (10)	91
Thomas Admans (11)	92
Jackson Cebula (11)	93
Devon Gledhill (10)	94
Megan Williams (9)	95

Springwood Federation (Junior School), Waterlooville

Felicity French (11)	96
Fynn Anthony Wyles (10)	97
Louise Wright (10)	98
Alfie Brian Jasper (10)	99
Phoebe Francis (11)	100
Eleanor Osgood (10)	101
Ellie Limburn (10)	102
Arlo Burnett (10)	103
Hollie McKenzie (10)	104
Nathan Peter Lee (10)	105
Aaliyah Cain (11)	106
Ethan Hunt (10)	107
Archie Tinsley (10)	108
Rosie Phillips (11)	109
Archie Stanley (11)	110
Jamie Morgan (11)	111
Rickey Denyer (11)	112

St Andrew's CE (VA) Primary School, Ecton Brook

Sarah Munga (10)	113
Victor Krzyzanowski (10)	114
Joshua Stewart (9)	115
Nicoletta Muraru (10)	116
Tia Cisovska (9)	117
Rutendo Muchachoma (10)	118
Stefan Andrei Ivan (10)	119
Andreea Puzderica (10)	120
Ariana Dumbrava (9)	121
Charlie Hartwell (9)	122
Harvey Olukomo (9)	123
Estelle Poku (9)	124
Tumise Shittu (9)	125
Riley-Ray Barrow (10)	126
Kayne Curry (9)	127
Divine Okwuchukwu (10)	128
Maja Szulczewska (9)	129

St George's Catholic Primary School, Sudbury Hill

Angel Bhardwaj (10)	130
Georgia Wozniak (9)	132
Harry Setchell (10)	133
Aahan Dangol (10)	134
Jan Kolankowski (10)	136
Gabriel Plusa (9)	137
James McLaughlin (9)	138
Stefania Bukala (9)	140
Mateusz Skrzynski (10)	141
Francis Osmani (9)	142
Maya Turner (10)	143
Amy Lorenzato (10)	144
Jayden Phillips-Clarke (9)	145
Adam Senftleben (10)	146
Eva Kedroe (10)	147
Tara Lama (9)	148
Hanna Wegrzyk (9)	149
Adrian Rajkumar (9)	150
Tyler Roche (9)	151
Angel Vijeyechandren (9)	152
Star Scarlett (10)	153
Aaron Lewis (10)	154
Clothilde Salord (10)	155
Alicja Prystasz (10)	156
Adriana Romanska (9)	157
Tymon Jankowicz (9)	158
George Coelho (10)	159
Freddie Thompson (9)	160
Riley Walter Jordan (9)	161
Arsenie Boca (10)	162
Julia Baran (9)	163
Charlize Yu (10)	164
Lena Kostuj (9)	165
Holly Masterson (9)	166
Olivia O'Leary (9)	167
Ayden Bonsu (9)	168
Josh (10)	169
Andre Khayrallah (10)	170
Kyron St Clair (10)	171

St Mary's Catholic Primary School, Gillingham

Sarah Hyland (10)	172
Victoria Irodalo (10)	174
Jacinta Barclay (9)	176
Melody Chang (10)	178
Ugochi Ikebudu (9)	180
Ilinca Honciuc (10)	181
Andrei Spinache (9)	182
Louis Dambreville-Harker (9)	183
Samuel Uzoegbu (10)	184
Chloe Chapman (10)	185
Osaremen Atoe (10)	186
Sophia Goulette (9)	187
Isaiah Nzau (10)	188
Annie-Rose Cornelius (9)	189
Jaiden Pitan (10)	190
Sariyah Davis (10)	191
Connie Brosnan (10)	192
Tabitha Brown (10)	193
Jakub Przybyla (9)	194
Grace Rajput (9)	195
Finley Elnaugh (9)	196
Ethan Redshaw (9)	197
Alexander Hales (10)	198
Chidubem Uche (9)	199
Greg Ehigie (9)	200
Kaima Eneh (10)	201
Chigozie Ejiofor (10)	202
Rhisiart Mabale (10)	203
Gargi Raote (9)	204
Kiril Rumiancev (10)	205
Aoife Lidsey (9)	206
Ryan Faradi (10)	207
Semilore Oluwatise (10)	208
Anthony Hilla (9)	209
Janica Barcelona (10)	210
Oliver Perez (9)	211
Kaden Banner (9)	212
Ollie Blee (9)	213
Sammy Major (10)	214
Jack Raymond Clark (9)	215
Beatrice Lapthorn (9)	216

Emmanuel David-Cole (10)	217
Zak Dempsay (10)	218
Sunny Ee (10)	219
Victor Emeakaroha (10)	220
Riley Peacock (9)	221
Mary-Lee Kempster (10)	222
Seren Roberts (10)	223
Adams Ojo (10)	224
Thomas Rose (9)	225
Michael Farrell (9)	226
Aaron Cuevas (10)	227
Tyler Harwood (10)	228
Jack Fordham (9)	229
Danielis Sirvinskas (9)	230
Albert Stanley (9)	231

St Vincent's RC Primary School, Dagenham

Sharon Akeju (10)	232
Saphron Serrant (10)	233
Philippa Kanneh (11)	234
Michaela Kondjo (10)	236
Marie-Lou Yenga (11)	237
Owen Orhue (11)	238
Gabriella Mazzon (11)	239
Sophie Perdoch (10)	240
Eghosa Ekhosuehi (11)	241
Rich Kodua (10)	242
Frederica Sackey (10)	243
Nathaniel Oluwasokale (11)	244
Michelle Nyarko (10)	245
Olatoye Oguntoye (10)	246
Lloyd Ackerson (11)	247
Paulina Geldon (10)	248
Peyton Cryillia Marina Shillingford (11)	249
Jimmy Wilkins (10)	250
Loraly Peta (10)	251
Ethan Doogan (10)	252
Kristian Marquez Ospina (11)	253
Mia Vaskeviciute (11)	254
Michael Oluyemi (10)	255

THE POEMS

A Star

You're a star, star, star
With your light shining bright
You flash like a lamp
And fly like a bird
When you're looking down
I'm looking up at you.
I twinkle just like you
And I look just like you.
You really are a star.

Jessica Emberson

Magic Me

Here are some things to note about me.
I love paddle-boarding and body-boarding in the sea.
I am not a big fan of school,
Although my friends there are really cool.
Harry Potter is all about me
But first comes my big family.
Oreos are my favourite snack,
And my best friends are called Herm, Tom, Charlie, Angus, Oscar, and Jack.
Angus is my friend and my dog,
He's a fox-red Lab, so he eats like a hog.
My two heroes are Daniel Radcliffe and Santa,
And every week when I go horse riding I like to canter.
On Minecraft and Roblox I'm a bit of a noob,
And I like to watch the Norris Nuts on YouTube.
For Christmas I got lots of Harry Potter Lego,
And I want to play with it so I might have to go.
In the library you'll find me in the J.K. Rowling section
Or listening to One Direction.

My name is Florence, yes I know,
But you can call me Floss or Flo.

Florence Hall (10)
Chantry Middle School, Morpeth

This Is Me!

Me,
As I curl my toes up in the blissful sand,
I feel the salty breeze calmly swooshing past me.
As I slowly bend back on the silky sand,
It feels like it's taking me away to the woods.
There I am.
The trees rustle,
I smell the youthful scent of pine saplings.
As I keep walking,
I hear the trickle of a waterfall bouncing against rocks and then slowly drifting off into the distance.
As I wander further into the calming forest, the soft trickle of the waterfall fades away.
I stand still... there I hear tweeting of birds high up.
And the soft squeak of mice scuttling around.
As I drift back to reality, the waves crash.
I smile.
This is my poem.
This is me.
And this is what I like.

Alice Leja (11)
Chantry Middle School, Morpeth

Me!

I get up every morning, I like to rise and shine.
I wonder what the day holds, through these eyes of mine.
I see the day, I want to play,
Many things get in the way.

I must get dressed, but what to wear?
I hate to choose and brush my hair.
I clean my teeth and wash my face,
There are sounds and smells all over the place.

My clothes feel strange, almost tight.
The thought of school gives me a fright.
So many kids, so much to do,
So many stairs, I can't be true!

I want to read the highway code,
Be with my pets - in my abode.
I need to cuddle,
And sort this muddle,
My brain so busy - I need a cuddle!

Evangeline (Evie) Ellery (10)
Chantry Middle School, Morpeth

Fear!

Ever felt shivers crawl up your back?
But then disappear when family has your back!
This is called fear, you can feel when he's near.

He makes you feel sad, it makes you scared,
Have a new fear? Be prepared!
He'll haunt the way you think,
But be scared to blink.

Don't let him get to you,
When he comes near, just say, "Shoo! Shoo!"
Tell him you're ready to love all fear!
This will scare him off, he'll never come near.
Ever felt shivers crawl up your back?

Lilly-Mae Wall (10)
Chantry Middle School, Morpeth

This Is Me!

B is for bookworm, as that's what I am.
E is for enjoys video games, and I am good at them as well.
N is for no fear when I rock climb.

Y is for yummy seafood, as that's what I like to eat.
O is for outstanding Lego sets as that's what I build.
U is for unlimited imagination which I use to tell stories.
N is for new experiences as that's what I like to try.
G is for great at board games, I play them all day.

Ben Young (11)
Chantry Middle School, Morpeth

Heidi's Acrostic Poem!

H appy, hilarious, and friendly, too!
E xcited, hard-working, and I enjoy school too!
I love journaling, reading, and watching Friends!
D reaming of being a journalist or maybe an author instead!
I enjoy swimming with the swim club, horse rising on Baz, and dancing at Zumba at the Saturday class!

Heidi Beale (10)
Chantry Middle School, Morpeth

You Are Unique

Remember you are unique.
No matter what anybody says, you are wonderful.
And if you can follow your dreams
Then you can be proud of who you are
If you struggle to remember this poem, always be yourself.
Remember, everyone is different.

Lillie Barton (10)
Chantry Middle School, Morpeth

This Is Me

This is me,
Football. Goal, goal, goal!
Newcastle United. Toon, Toon, black and white army.
Family, friends, mum, dad, sisters, uncle, auntie, grandma.
Video games. *Beep beep, pew pew.*
This is me!

Luke Smith (10)
Chantry Middle School, Morpeth

This Is Me

I am Ryan
Who is good at football
Who likes the colour orange
Likes to play Xbox
Enjoys eating chicken nuggets
Has friends named Freddie and Sam
And wants to learn more football.
This is me!

Ryan Humble (10)
Chantry Middle School, Morpeth

Being Eleanor

One cat.
One good night's sleep.
One giant bar of chocolate.
One summer's day.
One icy Fanta.
One action-packed theme park.
One big swimming pool.
One perfect day for me.

Eleanor Hodgson (11)
Chantry Middle School, Morpeth

All About Me

N ever betrayed people and never will
A lways brave like a tiger
D oesn't give up no matter what
I s eager to try new things
A lways try my hardest.

Nadia Rojek (11)
Chantry Middle School, Morpeth

My Recipe

Add lots of hugs,
Next add loads of happy.
After that, mix it and cook it for ten minutes.
Then pour excitedness,
And top it with a bit of funness,
This is me!

Alfie Egan (11)
Chantry Middle School, Morpeth

Back In A Year's Time

As the sun rises, the world awakes.
I went to school and did my work, nothing had changed to me.
I saw one of my favourite teachers.
I gave them a wave with glee, they taught me ICT for years.
Later that day she came to my class with news,
I thought it would be good like it usually would, but boy I was wrong.
She told us that she'd be gone for a year but was sure to come back.
In that moment my heart shattered like glass as I crumbled to the floor.
I felt the tension in the room grow and grow.
As she left to tell the other classes, we worked like normal,
But the aching pain inside me wouldn't go away,
It'd been a year now and she's back in the school.
But she'll never know how much we missed her.

Lucy Methven (11)
Coaltown Of Balgonie Primary School, Coaltown Of Balgonie

About Alex

Everybody thinks I'm amazing but I'm really just fun.
I have lots of friends and a big family, too.
I have a mum and a dad and they are so much fun.
I have a dog called Joey and a younger brother called Rory.
Everybody thinks I'm tall but I'm really not that tall.

Instead I'm kind of small.
I've got neat handwriting but sometimes I'm quite messy.
People think I'm responsible but I'm actually not that sensible.
People say I'm caring but I'm not good at sharing.

I like being organised so whatever I need to do I can do it.
I think I'm creative and people say I'm cool.
I am not that sensible, but I am really responsible.
I like to work hard so I can get my work done.
But I think I just do it to get school done.

Everyone says I run fast but I go faster on my motorbike.
I love motorbikes so much I would live on one.
People say I am fun but really I just like to run.

Alex Morrison (11)
Coaltown Of Balgonie Primary School, Coaltown Of Balgonie

A Poem About Me!

A lot of people say I'm smart but I don't agree with them,
I am not tall but I would describe myself as a flower stem,
I think this is because a lot of things are going round in my head,
And they're still there when I go to bed.

I'm described as amazing,
But really I'm just hardworking.
I like to get my work done and dusted,
No questions asked.

People think I'm responsible,
But I'm really not that sensible.
People say I'm caring,
But I'm not that good at sharing.

Most describe me as fun,
But I just like to run.
One day I want to fly through the sky,
But I'm just too shy.

Emma McGibbon (11)
Coaltown Of Balgonie Primary School, Coaltown Of Balgonie

Archie

Hi I'm Archie,
The clumsy one, the curious one, and even odd one,
All those things make me sound weird
And to that I'd say, you're right, I'm weird,
But honestly I wouldn't change a thing,
Because I like being weird 'cause it's not all the same thing.
One day it's gaming, the next day it's drawing.
Then it's my imagination, an entire constellation
A pinch of inspiration will make me go far,
Probably faster than a car on some tar.
So this is my rap about me,
So see you soon,
I hope you enjoyed my rap about me.

Archie Lawson (11)
Coaltown Of Balgonie Primary School, Coaltown Of Balgonie

This Is Me

R eally helpful to others at school and outside of school,
E verybody thinks I am very funny at school,
S uper active at dancing all the time.
P henomenal at most things,
O pen on ideas everywhere.
N ever give up on anything at all.
S uper good at art and drama.
I njure myself 24/7,
B eat Sabre is my favourite VR game,
L augh all the time at things that are not funny,
E diting is my favourite thing to do!

Kimberley Galloway (10)
Coaltown Of Balgonie Primary School, Coaltown Of Balgonie

I'm Proud

Scared of water,
Scared of skyscrapers.
Today I won't cry,
You can't blow me away.
I'm proud of myself just to say,
Even with a mask I'll keep breathing.
I'll strangle my fears so I don't have to meet them again.
I'll stay happy, even come rain.
I am myself, whatever you say I won't go insane.
Beels will roam out in spring mushrooms will always grow.
I love them so.

Lana Summers (11)
Coaltown Of Balgonie Primary School, Coaltown Of Balgonie

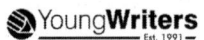

How To Be Friendly!

F orgiving is a part of me
R udeness can hurt others' feelings and is not a good thing to be
I nviting people into games is a nice thing to do
E ffective words do lots to make you cool
N eglect is something I would never do!
D etermined to finish a task
L eaving a warm feeling in your heart
Y early I can make you smile.

Aiden Melville (11)
Coaltown Of Balgonie Primary School, Coaltown Of Balgonie

Riddle Me This

I am tall in height but in width I could be short.
Sometimes I can look like a box that's been painted on without the same material.
There are decorations around me, I'm not alone.
I can also be similar to your home.
I offer a comfy bed and a warm welcoming retreat,
Come and get something to eat!
What am I?

Answer: A hotel.

Daniel Proctor (11)
Coaltown Of Balgonie Primary School, Coaltown Of Balgonie

My Feelings

My name is Harry and I'm a kind boy.
I have lots of friends that I like to annoy.
With my quirky sense of humour, I appear to be older than I am.
I enjoy playing my Xbox and riding my bike.
School is fun and interesting.
My favourite thing is science.
I dislike going on walks, it takes ages,
Like reading a book with lots and lots of pages.

Harry Good (10)
Coaltown Of Balgonie Primary School, Coaltown Of Balgonie

All About Me

This is all about me.
Sometimes my mam gives me the key.
My stepbrother annoys me and I really do mind it,
Whenever someone farts he says whoever rhymed it dimed it,
And I say whoever rhymed it did the crime.
And also my mum gets a Christmas tree and I always step on pines.
I always use the rivers that can bend.
Now I think this is the end.

Nicky Skinner (10)
Coaltown Of Balgonie Primary School, Coaltown Of Balgonie

This Is Me

L ovely
E ats chocolate all the time
X mas is my favourite season
I am funny and quick-reacting.

S afari parks are the best,
M y dog is crazy and never rests,
I am friendly and caring,
T ea and biscuits are very good,
H elping people like always.

Lexi Smith (11)
Coaltown Of Balgonie Primary School, Coaltown Of Balgonie

This Is Me!

D ance is my favourite thing,
A lthough it can get annoying.
N ow I have worked as hard as ever,
C oming every week like I have done forever.
I nteresting things every week,
N icola is my dance teacher, she sometimes makes me feel weak.
G ood and bad dance makes me glad.

Abbie McLaughlin (10)
Coaltown Of Balgonie Primary School, Coaltown Of Balgonie

Otis

C ool as freezing cold ice,
H elpful, happy, and nice.
E veryone thinks I'm cheerful and caring,
E veryone thinks I'm good at sharing.
R esponsible and peaceful,
F unny and careful.
U ncertain of most words and times,
L ikes to write a lot of lines.

Otis Leitch (11)
Coaltown Of Balgonie Primary School, Coaltown Of Balgonie

This Is Me

I'm a really big part in your heart
Even when we're apart.
I start with an F
I end with a Y.
When you're sad, I make you rise.
I am all different ages.
Sometimes old enough to pay wages.
I'll love you no matter what happens to you.
What am I?

Answer: Family.

Tianna Coppola (10)
Coaltown Of Balgonie Primary School, Coaltown Of Balgonie

Family

F amily is important
A family is with you for your whole life
M y family is really important to me
I can't imagine what it would be like without them
L ife with your family is amazing
Y our family is important and you should always love them.

Nicol Thomson (10)
Coaltown Of Balgonie Primary School, Coaltown Of Balgonie

This Is Me!

R idiculously crazy,
E nergetic like a car,
M ischievous in every situation,
I bend like a piece of paper.

W orthy of your time,
E ven if I can be annoying sometimes,
S peedy like the wind,
T imeless all the time.

Remi West (10)
Coaltown Of Balgonie Primary School, Coaltown Of Balgonie

My Dear Pops

Stars shine bright, I see you at night,
I can't hold my tears, I wish you were here,
Fearful I look into the dark night sky,
I see my emotions fly by,
I see you smile in my head,
You're not here in this world,
But you will always be in my heart.

Connor McLean (11)
Coaltown Of Balgonie Primary School, Coaltown Of Balgonie

Things About Me

P atient
H elpful
O rganised
T rusting
O pen-hearted
G raceful
R esourceful
A dventures
P henomenal
H onest
E nergetic
R espectful.

Campbell Jones (11)
Coaltown Of Balgonie Primary School, Coaltown Of Balgonie

This Is Me!

C ool and funny,
A mazingly strong.
M adly crazy, I have manners,
E ven while I'm really angry,
R ealistically uncontrollable,
O n the watch at all times,
N ever give up!

Cameron Melville (10)
Coaltown Of Balgonie Primary School, Coaltown Of Balgonie

My Favourite Person

V iolet is an exotic colour.
I nteresting like my gran.
O bliging, too.
L ovely and kind, everything nice.
E veryone loved her more than twice. I'm
T hankful for all my memories.

Stephen Wright (11)
Coaltown Of Balgonie Primary School, Coaltown Of Balgonie

Brooke

I am Brooke.

A mazing and kind,
M ean a little sometimes.

C aring and helpful,
O pen and trustworthy,
O rganised and reliable,
L oving and nice.

Brooke Jones (11)
Coaltown Of Balgonie Primary School, Coaltown Of Balgonie

This Is Me

O ften sporty and always funny like a clown
L ikeable like a showstar
L ike ice because I'm cool
Y oung and brave like a bear.

Olly Webster (11)
Coaltown Of Balgonie Primary School, Coaltown Of Balgonie

This Is Me!

When I make music it is so much fun
Someday I hope to be number one.
I like being loud and try to be heard
But nobody wants to hear.
I sit in my room every day,
I barely ever go out to play.
When my family listens I feel proud,
When I'm heard my inner self is found.
I love music. How much I'll never know.
I just like to let my spirit show.

Ffion Cross (10)
Craig Yr Hesg Primary School, Glyncoch

I Love My Mammy

Mammy is the best. I make the tea, she does the rest,
All the time she makes me food and does the chores,
She works every day without fail,
My mammy makes me happy.

Meals that my mammy give me are the best,
They are so yummy, you can tell because they go in my tummy.
You are the best mammy ever
And no matter what, I will always love you.

Olivia Stevens (10)
Craig Yr Hesg Primary School, Glyncoch

Why Horses Make Me Happy

H orses make me happy
O ur lives aren't complete without them
R iding horses is my favourite thing
S ame as when I stroke them.
E ven though they could possibly kill me, that isn't what matters
S eeing them every day and patting them every day would be the best.

Summer Griffiths (10)
Craig Yr Hesg Primary School, Glyncoch

Foster Carer

She looks after me,
Every single day.
She looks after me,
In every single way.
She looks after me,
When I fall down.
She looks after me,
When I may have a frown.
She looks after me,
To focus on my strengths.
She helps me achieve!
I will always love you.

Olivia Carter (9)
Craig Yr Hesg Primary School, Glyncoch

My Precious Pet

K ittens make me happy
I t's amazing to have one
T hey're cute and cuddly, like a pillow
T he sadness in her eyes makes my cry
E ven if you're down in the dumps they're here to cheer you up
N ice to see her when I come home.

Jacob Williams (10)
Craig Yr Hesg Primary School, Glyncoch

The Life Of Me

I will remember
That everyone I met cares for me
I will remember
That there will be a flare in my heart
I will remember
That I don't accept any dates
I will remember
There is a spot in the world for me
I will remember
My family will always be there.

Mason Davies (11)
Craig Yr Hesg Primary School, Glyncoch

What Makes Me Really Happy

H orses make me happy
O ur lives aren't complete without them
R eal happiness grows when I'm around them
S ame love with horses as with dogs
E ven riding them makes me overjoyed
S tanding next to them makes me the happiest.

Amelia Roberts (10)
Craig Yr Hesg Primary School, Glyncoch

Cuddly Kitten

K ittens make me happy
I t is the best to have one
T hey are quite loud but nice to take one
T hey're so cute and cuddle like a pillow
E ven down in the dumps she's there with me
N ice to see her when I am home.

Callum Bowns (10)
Craig Yr Hesg Primary School, Glyncoch

My Dream

M ammy is so pretty and she is the best
A mazing, she helps me if I'm crying
M ammy works hard and gets money
M usic is her favourite thing and
Y ellow is her favourite colour, and she is amazing and she loves me very much.

Lily May Hayman (10)
Craig Yr Hesg Primary School, Glyncoch

My Friend

S he makes me happy and she's my favourite, her eyes are bright.
U nbelievable kind to me,
M y friend is helpful to me.
M y friend plays with me.
E very day we play dogs.
R espects me wonderfully.

Olivia Stanton (9)
Craig Yr Hesg Primary School, Glyncoch

My Hero!

M y hero
A n angel
M y mum makes me smile,
M y mum is beautiful
Y ou will love my mum!

She takes care of me,
Like a mother on the run,
When she sits down,
She is back on the run.

Skye Baker (11)
Craig Yr Hesg Primary School, Glyncoch

Drawing Dream

D rawing is my safe zone
R elaxing in my bed as I draw
A rt is my soap
W ater arts are amazing
I n my mind as ideas go
N ow all done
G oing on a new adventure every day.

Zuzanna Bachula (11)
Craig Yr Hesg Primary School, Glyncoch

My Number One Dream

I have a dream.
I am standing on a stage.
I have a dream,
To go really far,
I have a dream,
To be one of a kind.
I have a dream,
The crowd will go loud.
I have a dream,
I am a famous singer.

Isobel Mardon-Hughes (10)
Craig Yr Hesg Primary School, Glyncoch

My Amazing Mum

She makes me
Happy and
She's my favourite,
Her eyes gleam
Bright as
The night.
Her clothes look pretty
And she's a witty,
She kisses me
And hugs me,
You are the best
Mum.

Ting Yan Harry Liu (9)
Craig Yr Hesg Primary School, Glyncoch

My Best Friend

O livia is my best friend in the world
L ike an angel in the big, bright sky
I love being around her
V ery nice
I am so happy she is my friend
A mazing heart.

Summer Green (10)
Craig Yr Hesg Primary School, Glyncoch

Heroes' Horizon

H eroes make me happy
E very day they help out
R acing to help others
O ver the buildings they leap
E very life must be helped
S aving lives is their routine.

Liam Richards (10)
Craig Yr Hesg Primary School, Glyncoch

All About My Best Friend

T he most wonderful friend ever
R espectful in every way
I mportant to me
C ares about me no matter what
E xciting to see
E xtraordinary in every single way!

Niamh Murphy (10)
Craig Yr Hesg Primary School, Glyncoch

My Dogs

M y dogs
Y ou will love my dogs.

D ogs I love
O nly I love as much as they love me
G o, my dogs are the best.
S ky, hi Sky, hi doggos, love me.

Olliver McGlennon (10)
Craig Yr Hesg Primary School, Glyncoch

My Precious Pet

F ull of joy.
U ses up all of my energy.
D ives into everything.
G ets into the food cupboard every day.
E very day he makes me smile.

Grace Morgan (9)
Craig Yr Hesg Primary School, Glyncoch

My Best Friend

G rateful for everything she gets
R espectful with others
A wesome with everything
C areful for others
E xtra nice to other people.

Phyllisity Hawkins (11)
Craig Yr Hesg Primary School, Glyncoch

All About My Brother

R espectful and always there for me
O utstanding
B rave
B ro
I mportant to me
E xtraordinary.

Thomas Griffiths (10)
Craig Yr Hesg Primary School, Glyncoch

This Is Me

I am Raafi Hasan,
I'm nine in Year Five;
I'm even a human being,
In June I will be ten,
And I'm short as a mouse.

I like monkeys,
Because they're as fast as a hare.
I even like anime;
Because I like to watch them fight,
My favourite character is Goku,
Because he's as strong as a gorilla.

In my spare time,
I would clean my room until its clean as a pond,
Or I would play Rocket League learning
how to air-dribble.

Once I am older,
I would like to be an animator or a footballer,
If I became an animator I would name
my anime Fusuki,
If I were a footballer I would join Liverpool.

Raafi Hasan (9)
Gardners Lane Primary School, Cheltenham

This Is Me

I am adventurous
I've seen Burj Khalifa
And his little brother Burj Araf
Also Big Ben
And parliament. I wander and wander
like a stray cat.

I love to game on my Xbox
And play Fortnite on and on
Also buy clothes to wear
And my favourite of them all is Turkish ice cream.

I'm good at gaming
Football
Flipping on my trampoline
Making friends.

I'd like to be a streamer when I'm older
Or a businessman to be cooler than
Cool Ranch Doritos
I'd like to be a star getting flashed by many lights.

Adrin Murshed (9)
Gardners Lane Primary School, Cheltenham

This Is Me

This is me, amazing Ahsan,
I live in Cheltenham,
I have two brothers and one sister,
I'm fun and a good friend.

In my spare time, it's PS4 time,
My PS4 is like a mansion,
My games are Minecraft,
I'm very grateful for my PS4.

I'm good at Beanie Wars,
Me and my friend created it and he is a star,
It was too easy to beat him,
And beat his record.

In the future I want to be a banker,
So I could get a lot of money,
And give it to charity,
Because I'm a good person.

Ahsan Uddin (9)
Gardners Lane Primary School, Cheltenham

Jumpy James

I'm a brother, an older brother
I like to play on my laptop or PS4
Violent things are my game
As I like to beat my brother in a round of Jumpforce

I can be as nice as a playful puppy
But I could also be as angry as a dragon
I have a certain set of limits for my anger
So you'll never know when I'll burst

I also like to help with cooking
But when it's spaghetti I get a bit excited
As it's the best dish there could ever be
Chomp! Chomp! Down you go.

James Holloway (10)
Gardners Lane Primary School, Cheltenham

This Is Magnificent Miley

Lying under the tree
Thoughts running through her head
Amazing as she seems
Joyful as she plays

She waits and waits, nothing ever happens
But her smile never goes away
She's feisty, she cares
But trouble always comes first

Some people call her magnificent Miley
She's funny, she's helpful and tidy
That's why I have lots of friends
This is magnificent Miley and that's that.

Miley Hornby (11)
Gardners Lane Primary School, Cheltenham

This Is The Mysterious Me!

At school, I am a shy girl,
A girl that knows everything,
But doesn't say anything.

Outside with my friends, I am very funny,
And I make myself look smart and shiny.

At home, I am very mysterious,
I sometimes cry for no reason,
Or get excited for only a season.

Most of the time, I am creative,
I sometimes can be calculating.

That's why this is the mysterious me!

Melany Del Cid Aguirre (10)
Gardners Lane Primary School, Cheltenham

This Is Terrible Tyler

Hey I'm terrible Tyler
And I like certain games
One of them is football
And my favourite colour is yellow

My friends say I'm funny
But I don't think I am
My favourite food is pasta
I'm a big brother of two, they all love me

I have a lot of friends
Because I'm helpful, kind and caring
And people say I'm a smart boy
This is terrible Tyler and that's it.

Tyler Finn (10)
Gardners Lane Primary School, Cheltenham

This Is Me!

I am Riyad. I'm a student, I'm friendly,
Funny, annoying, fun, and adventurous.
I'm a Muslim. I'm as busy as a busy bee!

I like to play Roblox with my friends.
I like having trips because I'm as adventurous as a plane.
I like eating food.
I like making people laugh.
I like technology.

I'm good at games.
I'm good at technology.
I'm good at predicting.

Riyad Shalahin (9)
Gardners Lane Primary School, Cheltenham

Me

I'm the girl sat next to you
People describe me as chatty and confident
Pretty and smart

But I'm really different inside
I'm actually insecure and quiet
Not many people know but I have lost my mom

I am a sister
I am a friend
I am a pupil
And last of all I am a human

Loyal Libby
Lovely Libby
I am Libby
The one and only me!

Libby Lewis-Hall (11)
Gardners Lane Primary School, Cheltenham

This Is Me

There is a positive person here,
Who always is a fun tear.
She's grinning all the time,
This is such a lovely rhyme!

She jokes all around,
She might fall down!
She won't take no for an answer,
Unless somebody tells her.

This girl won't let anybody down,
If she does, she might have a frown,
Yes, this girl is me,
Why can't anyone see?

Kiana Aswat (10)
Gardners Lane Primary School, Cheltenham

Skye's Fun Life

Hi, my name is Skye,
I have seven siblings,
And they are caring and funny,
My mum and dad are funny as well.

I like writing stories and poems,
And I am excited to go to secondary,
Also, my SATs are soon,
I have four budgies.

I have make-up, my own bedroom,
And my house is very busy.
I am happy that I get to see,
My friends at school.

Skye Clarke (11)
Gardners Lane Primary School, Cheltenham

This Is Me

Hi, my name is Ana.
And I am a student.
It is fun to come to school.
And have fun with my friends.

I'm good at gymnastics,
Like a monkey swinging in the trees.
I like chocolate and chips.
My favourite thing to do is art and eating apples.

I'm friendly and happy all the time.
I want to be when I grow up is a flight attendant.

Ana Maria (9)
Gardners Lane Primary School, Cheltenham

The Cool Car

Hi my name is Carson
A chattery chatterbox
I'm sometimes annoying and also shy
I need to build enough courage to say hi

I like eating eggs
I prefer them scrambled
Like my brave bro's brain
In a test

I really like games
They are a bunch of flames
But I always leave my room in a mess
Like a just had a feast.

Carson (10)
Gardners Lane Primary School, Cheltenham

Hi I'm Awesome Oscar

I'm awesome Oscar
I like to play football
Like my idol Salah
Who plays for Liverpool

I'm a joyful brother
Helping my brother doing his homework
Boring, boring, not fun, not fun
Finished finally, let's go and play

Also I like to go to school
Playing with friends
Playing football
I'm awesome Oscar.

Oscar Lightstone (10)
Gardners Lane Primary School, Cheltenham

Decisive Daizzy

I'm a picky person
A not friendly one
I don't eat much
But I love taking pictures

I love all types of dancing
As much as you could think of
I am very competitive
When it comes to me

I always love challenges
Because without it I won't overcome anything
I am a very girly one
And a sister of all.

Daizzy Njoku (11)
Gardners Lane Primary School, Cheltenham

Talktative Ifra

I'm Ifra
A friendly face
I like to sleep and eat sweets
Yum, yum, yum!

I'm not very patient
Like a hungry lion
I like to hang out with my friendly friends
I'm a helpful sister

I'm into watching movies and
I like to go to theatres
I'm as quiet as a mouse but
I can be as big as a house.

Ifra Rahman (11)
Gardners Lane Primary School, Cheltenham

Marvellous Maisie

Hi my name is Maisie
I love going to school
My favourite food is chocolate
Dark and smooth

My favourite animal is a zebra
All black and white
I love playing with friends
They're really kind!

I'm a friendly chatterbox
As patient as a cat
A caring, loving sister
I'm Maisie and that's that!

Maisie Hester (10)
Gardners Lane Primary School, Cheltenham

About Me!

I'm a lovely Oliwia
I love to read books
Reacting to stories about animals
As fast as a cheetah

I'm a super sister
Helping Mum entertain
Making him giggle
Makes me joyful

I'm marvellous me
I like to eat chocolate
It's delicious and tasty
Munch, munch, crunch, crunch.

Oliwia Czajkowska (10)
Gardners Lane Primary School, Cheltenham

Jolly Jed

I am a friendly friend
I like warm hugs like a teddy bear
I play football like Ronaldo
I am as fast as a cheetah

I like eating ice cream
Hmm, hmm, hmm,
Smooth like chocolate
A caring, helpful brother

I love playing football
And going out shopping
As patient as a saint
A loving friend.

Jedidiah Adedipe (10)
Gardners Lane Primary School, Cheltenham

Friendly Paige

I live with my brother and my mother
I like playing with my brother
Hugging my mother
I am good at English

Good at SPaG
I am a sweet and kind person
It always fills me up inside
When I see my brother happy

I am as playful as a baby cub
I am a cuddly, loving sister.

Paige Jackson (10)
Gardners Lane Primary School, Cheltenham

This Is Me

I am
Kind and loving
Like a panda
Bear.

One of my favourite fun
Sports is football
As a goalkeeper
The other jobs I
Despair.

I'm like
An artist when
I'm doing
Art.

When I'm older
I would like
To be very
Strong.

Scarlett-Mai James (9)
Gardners Lane Primary School, Cheltenham

Me In A Nutshell

I'm amazing Archie
I like being sociable
Like a busy butterfly
Or a buzzing bee

I'm a helpful brother
Like a terrific teacher
Telling them about space
And superb science

A loving hug for Mum
A helping hand for Dad
And most of all
I'm Archie!

Archie Orpin (10)
Gardners Lane Primary School, Cheltenham

This Is Me

I am a smiling sister
I am a delicate daughter
I am kind, funny and smart
I am caring to others

I am like a warm teddy bear
Leaping towards you
I am a warm-hearted
Loving person

I am a graceful grandaughter
I am a like a bundle of kindness
This is me.

Evie Davis (10)
Gardners Lane Primary School, Cheltenham

This Is Me!

Smart at science,
Marvellous at maths,
Kind and keen,
Full of smiles.

I want to be a lawyer,
I want to help people in trial,
Dark chocolate eyes,
Friendly face.

Fun and funny,
Enthusiastic and eager,
Pleasant and passionate,
Jubilant and jolly.

Srinika Pesaladinne (10)
Gardners Lane Primary School, Cheltenham

This Is Me

An ambitious, gentle person,
Like daisies in the soil.

A loving person,
With a beautiful imagination.

Like a ballerina on stage with pride,
And a huge smile on her face.

Wild and jubilant,
With an adventurous story to tell.

Ayo
Gardners Lane Primary School, Cheltenham

This Is Sayu

I'm Sayu
I'm soft and warm
Like a teddy bear

I like maths
And I'm good
Like a teacher

My favourite food
Is pizza
I love to play football
And I'm good like
Cristiano Ronaldo.

Sayu Sasikumar (11)
Gardners Lane Primary School, Cheltenham

Me

This is me
A fast boy
I like to play Roblox

My friends say
That I am
Kind, helpful, funny
The fastest runner

I like to play
Build up tag with my friends
Have a great day.

Archie Locke (9)
Gardners Lane Primary School, Cheltenham

I Have A Dream

I have a dream that I could be a hero,
But bad dreams and doubts can make me feel like a zero,
I am creative but I never know where to start,
Pens and pencils storm my desk, lighting up a spark in my mind of deep, deep, dark,
I love the outdoors, playing football with my friends,
The fun just never ends.

I have a dream to build a Lego city,
But every time I go online, everyone else's are ten times better,
I am persistent in my dreams and goals,
Like saving a goal for England,
And being super famous,
Maybe make my own trainers, Michael Jordans.

I have to dream to win as a poet, I just know it.

Max Perett-King (11)
Mears Ashby CE Primary School, Mears Ashby

My Dream

This is me, I'm brave and proud
This is me, I'm kind and loving
This is me, I'm caring and loud
This is me, I'm in the zone.

Every day I ride and play
Every day I read and game
Every day I care and lay
Every day I love my family.

This is me, I'm the smallest of them all
This is me, I'm the youngest of them all
Every day I love and pray
Every day I love my family!

Olivia Preston (10)
Mears Ashby CE Primary School, Mears Ashby

Embarrassing

Embarrassing,
Well, that's what my brothers think,
I scruff their hair, embarrassing,
I give them a hug, embarrassing,
I talk to them, *embarrassing!*
I'm starting to think it's my new name.
But! I take this as pride, I know,
To be a good sibling you need to be annoying!

Yours sincerely,
Embarrassing Big Sister.

Brooke Browne (11)
Mears Ashby CE Primary School, Mears Ashby

Love

I am the love of your life
You can count on me like one, two, three, I'll be there
You'll always smile
You'll never be down
I'll never leave you, never ever
I'll be there forever and ever
I'll cheer you on
I'll keep you going
I'll give you happiness
Love.

Jess Cooling (10)
Mears Ashby CE Primary School, Mears Ashby

Happiness And Love

I am the light of your heart
I will keep you smiling
I will always be with you
I will always have your back
I will never leave
I count your heartbeat, one, two, three
I am all that you will be
I am the one who can fix anything
I give you lots of energy.

Sophia Sargent (9)
Mears Ashby CE Primary School, Mears Ashby

Me!

Everywhere I go,
I like being me,
The people that I love,
Are in my family!
My favourite food is cheese,
I really like it plain,
Whenever I eat it,
I always go insane!
My name is Elijah,
I'm very smart,
One of my dreams,
Is to drive a go-kart!

Elijah Borbor (10)
Mears Ashby CE Primary School, Mears Ashby

Me

My name is Tommy
I write really neat
When someone raps
I have a great beat.

I play football
With my friends
Our friendship
Will never end.

I play Xbox
I've got a new controller
And I don't want to be a bowler.

Thomas Admans (11)
Mears Ashby CE Primary School, Mears Ashby

Football

I am respect, passion and sensation
All in one, I slowly trickle through
Your veins and produce magic.
I make people happy and sad.
I am people's life, I can ruin it or make it.
I am football.

Jackson Cebula (11)
Mears Ashby CE Primary School, Mears Ashby

Me Is Me

D are-devil Devon
E nergised, biking along the streets
V ery into my Switch
O rganised, orange
N ice, paradise, rice.

Devon Gledhill (10)
Mears Ashby CE Primary School, Mears Ashby

This Is Me

Woke up at 11:30am
Feeling like I can do anything
Go to rugby
Have lots of fun
Then go home and
Exercise.

Megan Williams (9)
Mears Ashby CE Primary School, Mears Ashby

Felicity French

Cheeky, chatty, clumsy, that's always me,
I have many nicknames, including Fee.
Pantos are my thing, look, he's behind you!
Dawn French is one of my relatives, too.
Cats, fish, and guinea pigs are what I own,
I make sure that they are never alone.
Gabrielle's my best friend - Brie Brie for short,
Dance is mine and my friends' favourite sport.
The songs that I love are sung by Adele,
I like Tom Holland, but don't go and tell!
I have bright blue eyes and golden brown hair,
My brother's annoying - let's not go there.
I'm a puppy as playful as can be,
Enjoy this poem to celebrate me!

Felicity French (11)
Springwood Federation (Junior School), Waterlooville

Fynn Wyles

My name's Fynn and I love to play football,
I have lots of friends, but I'm very small.
I have lots of family, yes I do!
I love eating ice cream, and chocolate too!
Playing Minecraft and Roblox is so fun,
I hate sports day because I have to run.
I have two sisters and a small brother,
I have a father and a nice mother!
I have two grandads, I have two nannies,
I don't call them grampas nor them grannies!
I have two pets named Bella and Gingy,
I have lots of clothes, which are not cringy!
I have many more games called It Takes Two.
Everyone calls me Fynny, do you too?

Fynn Anthony Wyles (10)
Springwood Federation (Junior School), Waterlooville

Louise

Drawing and playing, I'm a crafty one.
Screaming and yelling, I do that for fun!
The stars in the night sky, I love to draw,
Imagine an astronaut, would see more.
Don't be fooled by their eyes, red, brown, and white,
Red pandas are their name, but they won't bite.
Lotus biscuits, my favourite with tea.
I will be kind, so you can share with me.
Cookie Run Kingdom, the best game I play.
I will turn eleven this year, hooray!
I am a puppy, hyper and funny!
My dream pet is a fluffy, black bunny.
The family Madrigal is the best!
And North Columbia is warm like West!

Louise Wright (10)
Springwood Federation (Junior School), Waterlooville

Alfie

Hi, I like to play a game called football,
A lot of people know that I am small.
I'm always happy and energetic.
If you are sad, I am sympathetic.
I like to play Minecraft and FIFA too,
If you want to know more, this is a clue:
I've got two dogs and five puppies. So what!
I like to eat meatloaf because it is hot!
I always play on Bandlab Music too,
Someone, born in twenty-eleven, who?
I have two dads and five brothers, that's true!
I like to colour and the best is blue!
Pouncing with energy, I am a dog.
I do not like sports day; I hate to jog!

Alfie Brian Jasper (10)
Springwood Federation (Junior School), Waterlooville

Phoebe Francis

I am a hyena, headstrong and proud,
I am sometimes quiet but always loud,
I'm Phoebe and I'm eleven years old,
I play rugby even with it is cold,
My hopes and dreams are to be horse riding,
I like to stand out instead of hiding.
Five horses, and three pigs, four oaks, two snails,
They are my pets and they mostly have tails.
Archie, Finley, Josie, Daryl, Daisy,
We go out when I don't feel as lazy.
Scarlett and Aaliyah, they are the best,
On most days they put my patience test.
My personality crazy can be,
I am Phoebe Francis and this is me!

Phoebe Francis (11)
Springwood Federation (Junior School), Waterlooville

Eleanor

My personality is really kind.
My favourite show is something I can find.
I like to play Roblox on my laptop,
I really dislike popcorn that goes pop.
One of my friends is sometimes called Nicole.
Sometimes we try to put her in a hole.
I have lots of rabbits that mostly bite.
Without my glasses on I lose my sight.
My three birds are very stinky and loud.
Sometimes my writing makes me very proud.
If I get in trouble, I sometimes lie.
If my sister gets mad at me, I sigh.
At school break time I like to climb up high.
My name is Eleanor, for now bye-bye!

Eleanor Osgood (10)
Springwood Federation (Junior School), Waterlooville

Ellie

I'm a Cancer, born in the month of July,
When I'm naughty, most of the time, I lie.
I am a ten-year-old girl with a cat.
My best friend calls my pet gerbil a rat.
My favourite food is pasta with cheese.
If my sister annoys me, I will tease.
I want to be part of the NHS.
If you enter my room, you will see a mess.
My dad is proud with the way that I act.
I am lazy now, that is a true fact.
Most of the time I am weird and funny.
I prefer the weather if it's sunny,
I'm a monkey, cheeky, and devious.
When I am angry, I'm mischievous.

Ellie Limburn (10)
Springwood Federation (Junior School), Waterlooville

Arlo Burnett

I would love to be a pro footballer.
Every day, my friends say I get smaller.
The football team I support is Pompey,
I have a best friend he is called Ronnie.
I am Pisces, in the month of March.
My mum and dad have a good, thoughtful heart.
I have a big, fluffy dog called Maia,
In the winter, she sits by the fire.
I'm a cheetah, energetic and fast,
Who knows how long my energy will last.
I am now ten, my digits are double,
Trying my best to stay out of trouble.
I like to draw because that's what I do,
The ocean, my favourite colour, blue.

Arlo Burnett (10)
Springwood Federation (Junior School), Waterlooville

Hollie

I am an Aries, born in the month of March.
My heart is big, it has a giant arch.
I am Hollie, my nickname is HollsDolls,
But my family like to call me Holls.
Singing with piano is what I like.
My favourite shoe brand ever is Nike.
An actress I would like to be one day.
Films and TV or sometimes a good play,
Harry Potter, Hermoine Granger,
Voldemort causes all of the danger.
My brother calls me moody, that's a fact,
But only when he says I cannot act.
I'm a celebrity, kind and well-dressed,
The TV show Friends is what I know best.

Hollie McKenzie (10)
Springwood Federation (Junior School), Waterlooville

Nathan

My best friends call me by my nickname, Nate.
In my family my dad is my mate.
I like to re-read my favourite book.
Most days I ask my mum if I can cook.
The place I love to eat is McDonald's.
I like to visit my grandad Ronald.
I love to play FIFA Ultimate Team.
My best friend Christian was in my dream.
I'm a Taurus born in the month April.
On pancakes, I use the syrup maple.
When we go to Ikea, we don't buy.
During a school play, I am very shy.
I am a giraffe, very tall and loud.
I got a high score in my test, I'm proud!

Nathan Peter Lee (10)
Springwood Federation (Junior School), Waterlooville

Aaliyah

I am a star, independent and strong,
Love Harry Potter, could read all day long.
I love to watch the midnight stars alone.
Peace, quiet, I even switch off my phone.
I love summertime, when the flowers bloom.
Their beautiful colours brighten a room!
I love slow sloths, cute, fluffy, and small.
Unlike them I don't climb trees I may fall.
Shepherd's pie, gravy, peas, are so yummy.
My favourite fidget is a Poppit,
My favourite necklace type is a locket,
I like to eat lots and lots of gummies!
The best are the bears, that taste of honey!

Aaliyah Cain (11)
Springwood Federation (Junior School), Waterlooville

Ethan

My name is Ethan, I like game playing
Football, Roblox, you know what I'm saying
I am a little sloth, lazy, and slow
I do, however, give things a good go
A software engineer I'd like to be
That is the future, from what I can see
Macaroni cheese, my favourite dish
My mum prepares it whenever I wish
My favourite music is rock and pop
My mum shouts at me whenever it has to stop
Bowling and the beach, a family treat
Camping under the stars, you cannot beat
I'm a little shy, but I do like to join in
I play games, I like to win.

Ethan Hunt (10)
Springwood Federation (Junior School), Waterlooville

Archie Tinsley

I'm a broken record, I always talk.
And at school break time, I take a small walk.
My favourite game is to play football.
Everybody knows that I am quite small.
You can agree, I can be very loud.
You should know now, I can be very proud.
I even have a cute little pet pug.
I bought a painting instead of a hug.
I like to play FIFA 22 draft.
And a pixel game that is called Minecraft.
My football team is Liverpool FC.
I shall support them for eternity.
I have a pet hamster that bit my hand.
I am the smartest Tinsley in this land.

Archie Tinsley (10)
Springwood Federation (Junior School), Waterlooville

Rosie

Hi, I am ten and my name is Rosie.
I love my home, it is very cosy.
I don't like Covid, but I love the sea.
I like winter because it is icy.
I like to play with my little puppy.
But he rolls in the mud and gets mucky.
I go ice skating every Saturday,
I started in 2018 in May.
I am saving up to buy a pet fish.
Chocolate ice cream is my favourite dish.
My favourite thing is now history,
It's because it is all a mystery.
Well, this was fun, hope you learned something new.
I really hope I win, what about you?

Rosie Phillips (11)
Springwood Federation (Junior School), Waterlooville

Archie

Archie
Ten years ago
I was born, blonde and cool
I am a snake, my friends call me Arch
My friends.

My friends
Fun and awesome
Basketball with Jamie
We are like the Chicago Bulls
Good food.

Good food
I like all foods
Spicy wings, prawns, and fish
Also I like to drink Fanta
That's me.

Archie Stanley (11)
Springwood Federation (Junior School), Waterlooville

Jamie

Jamie
Ten years ago
I was born in London
My friends call me Jammie Dodger

My dogs
Cute and fluffy
They are clumsy and fun
My dogs are golden Labradors

Love food
McDonald's, yum
Oasis and burger
It's my favourite food and drink
That's me.

Jamie Morgan (11)
Springwood Federation (Junior School), Waterlooville

Ricky

Ricky
I'm eleven
I like to eat pizza
I am a monkey, cheeky, fun
Boxing.

Boxing
I love boxing
I like to play football
I have a dog called Apollo
Sister.

Sister
I have a sister
I love Marvel movies
I watch movies with my sister
Chatty.

Rickey Denyer (11)
Springwood Federation (Junior School), Waterlooville

Sunday Morning

I wake up every morning with a groan,
When I realise I have school,
All I do is moan.
Then I remember it's Sunday,
I jump around on my bed,
And let out a big, "Yay!"

I'll put on my best dress,
Find my cold necklace,
And I'll figure out the rest.
Now it's almost time to go,
But before I leave,
There's something you should know.

I love being with my friends,
'Cause when I'm with them,
The fun never ends.
They're always there for me,
No matter what,
They'll always accept what I'll be.

Sarah Munga (10)
St Andrew's CE (VA) Primary School, Ecton Brook

The Wonderful Me

If I had to trade places with someone,
I don't know who I'd be.
This is because I don't want to be anyone,
Except for the wonderful me.
I am weird, fun, and most importantly, kind,
And if you're ever in trouble,
I'll keep you in mind.
I'm as playful as a panther
And as energetic as an eel,
And if you ever need a friend,
I'll be one that is real.
If I had to trade places with someone,
I don't know who I'd be.
This is because I don't want to be anyone,
Except for the wonderful me.

Victor Krzyzanowski (10)
St Andrew's CE (VA) Primary School, Ecton Brook

If I Was Food

I am a curious cake,
A teaspoon of cheekiness,
A sprinkle of worries,
And a cup of smartness.

I am a scrumptious chocolate bar,
As sweet as a Haribo,
I'm as good as I could be,
I love the wonderful me.

I am a delightful doughnut,
An animal lover,
I've held a couple of scary creepy-crawlies,
Such as tarantulas, Chinese stick insects, and an African snail.

Joshua Stewart (9)
St Andrew's CE (VA) Primary School, Ecton Brook

This Is Nicoletta!

N ice as a nurse.
I love to go to Romania.
C onfident in myself.
O n the aeroplane with my pets.
L oving as a mother caring for her children.
E veryone likes me for who I am.
T otally clumsy, but only sometimes.
T ry my hardest in everything.
A s fast as a dog.

Nicoletta Muraru (10)
St Andrew's CE (VA) Primary School, Ecton Brook

I Am A Cake

I am a cake,
A spoon of love,
A cup of hope,
With all of this, a dash of ambition.

A sprinkle of curiosity,
A pinch of joy,
A bowl of fun snowballs,
And a handful of peace.

A spoon to stir,
A bowl of heart,
An oven to cook me,
And all of these ingredients make all of me.

Tia Cisovska (9)
St Andrew's CE (VA) Primary School, Ecton Brook

How To Make Me Recipe

R aindrops of small happiness
U nlimited amounts of boredom
T iny sprinkles of friends
E very colour I think of is black and white
N ever-ending sadness
D ashes of kindness
O nly feels confident sometimes.

M y friends and family make me smile.

Rutendo Muchachoma (10)
St Andrew's CE (VA) Primary School, Ecton Brook

This Is Me

I'm tall but still quite small,
I'm a tiger ready to pounce,
I'm easy to startle but not at most measly,
I'm a little mischievous,
I'm a rat,
You let me free, I'll get into places I shouldn't,
I'm skinny as a stick,
I love me because it's just me!

Stefan Andrei Ivan (10)
St Andrew's CE (VA) Primary School, Ecton Brook

This Is Me

A dream of mine is to help all the poor animals.
N ice to other people.
D ogs are nice and cute.
R omania is a good country, like others.
E nglish is the language we speak.
E mpathy is the school value.
A malia is one of my best friends.

Andreea Puzderica (10)
St Andrew's CE (VA) Primary School, Ecton Brook

This Is Me!

A mazing, awesome, and generous,
R ipened peaches are my favourite.
I love hanging out with mates,
A malia and Andreea are their names.
N ot the best with reality,
A s I'm always stuck in an eternal daydream.

Ariana Dumbrava (9)
St Andrew's CE (VA) Primary School, Ecton Brook

This Is Me

C ars are my favourite
H aribos are my favourite
A nswers I check
R iley-Ray is my best friend
L ove football because it makes you fit
I love football more than a fish loves water
E nglish is good.

Charlie Hartwell (9)
St Andrew's CE (VA) Primary School, Ecton Brook

All About Me

F ast and courageous
A lso annoying
N ice to my friends
T ender and kind
A nd sometimes silly
S peedy and quick
T hinks a lot about future
I ntelligent
C reative and cool.

Harvey Olukomo (9)
St Andrew's CE (VA) Primary School, Ecton Brook

I Love Me The Way I Am

I'm tall
I'm funny
I'm happy
Like a bunny.
I'm nice
I'm kind
I'm fast
Like a dart.
My hair is
Fluffy like a cloud.
My eyes are brown
Like the ground.
I love me
The way
I am.

Estelle Poku (9)
St Andrew's CE (VA) Primary School, Ecton Brook

Sour Apple

Laughter and fun, a smile makes me jump;
Cakes and chicken, too scrumptious to eat.
With a word to make you smile, you'll be a better person.
Being weird is nothing to worry about,
So stop looking down and don't be a sour apple!

Tumise Shittu (9)
St Andrew's CE (VA) Primary School, Ecton Brook

This Is Riley-Ray Barrow

B rave as a lion,
A dream of mine is to be a professional motocross rider,
R acing through the sky high,
R iley-Ray Barrow,
O n his Mad 4 Motocross motorbike,
W heeling through the finish.

Riley-Ray Barrow (10)
St Andrew's CE (VA) Primary School, Ecton Brook

This Is Me

To make me, you will need:
An eruption of laughter
A bus of mischief
A river of fun
An ocean of silliness
A spoonful of sadness
A sprinkle of curiosity
A mansion of rage.

Kayne Curry (9)
St Andrew's CE (VA) Primary School, Ecton Brook

This Is Me!

D ivine is my name
I love Christmas
V ery mischievous
I liked to read Dork Diaries
N oodles are my favourite food
E verything should be pink.

Divine Okwuchukwu (10)
St Andrew's CE (VA) Primary School, Ecton Brook

How To Make Me

M assive spoon of happiness.
A spoonful of boredom.
J ug of excitement.
A handful of paint.

Maja Szulczewska (9)
St Andrew's CE (VA) Primary School, Ecton Brook

All About Me

M y favourite animal is a dog
C ats aren't cool with me
D on't ever be sad, be happy
O livia, Sara, James, and Josh are my best friends
N ando's is a no, McDonald's to go
A ngel is my name
L ove maths
D ogs are my life
S uper sneaky is my superpower.

B rilliant, superb, those are my words
I ntelligence, independent, these desirable friends
G irls rule, boys don't

D on't doubt me
O ranges and apples are my favourite fruits
U se my silliness
B ingo, I have a lingo
L ove my neighbours
E erie is a noise

D ogs are the cutest animals
E mily is my puppy's name
C an you sing? No, I can't
K eep safe
E llie is my outside school best friend
R ight I am always.

B ut not perfect
I gniting pinks are my favourite colour
G eorge is the longest friend we've known.

M cDonald's is my favourite
A pples on the go
C an I please win.

Angel Bhardwaj (10)
St George's Catholic Primary School, Sudbury Hill

This Is Me!

Here is a poem to get to know about me...

T hings I love - reading, school, and hobbies.
H appy, funny, and maybe a comedian.
I love my dogs.
S porty, likes gymnastics, football, and tennis.

I have a great family.
S ometimes I can be hyper but I never stop.

M y favourite colours are blue and red.
E lephants aren't my favourite animal.

G lasses I don't wear, but I have blue eyes.
E lla, Rebekah, and Frankie, they're my sisters.
O thers think I'm loud.
R eally, I'm very smart, passionate, and chilled.
G oing to school every day with my mum and dad except the weekend.
I dol is Adele (I love her).
A nd - this is me!

Georgia Wozniak (9)
St George's Catholic Primary School, Sudbury Hill

Who Am I?

H ard-working and trying to stay focused
A mazing in my own way
R eally loves football
R emember what my parents do for me
Y ellow waffles, one of my favourite foods.

S porty and silly, that's how I roll
E xcitable, especially at parties or in football crowds
T ottenham Hotspur, their number one fan
C reative, and a large chocolate fan
H undreds of football cards at home
E nergetic, always running around
L ikes school especially, physical education, maths, and poetry
L ights up my home. This is me.

Harry Setchell (10)
St George's Catholic Primary School, Sudbury Hill

This Is Me, Aahan!

My name is Aahan,
I am a genius boy.
I am bold and fearless,
I don't play with a toy.

My favourite movie is Spider-Man,
I'm a gigantic fan.
I'm a very good fighter,
But not a good biter.

I am Aahan,
The most enthusiastic boy you'll ever meet.
My eye colour is brown,
That is why I don't carry a frown.

I want to be adventurous,
Climb up tall towers.
No matter if it is treacherous,
I might find more powers.

I am passionate,
For who I am,
I am also eager and chatty.

This is me!

Aahan Dangol (10)
St George's Catholic Primary School, Sudbury Hill

Jan Is The Plan

T his is me, Jan!
H ere are foods I like: pizza, burgers, and meat.
I don't know which food is better. Burgers or pizza?
S howing my positive aura spreads like an infection.

I like computers and Among Us.
S ome other things I like are computers and toy guns (Nerf and X-Shot).

M y family gave me a Nintendo Switch for Christmas.
E very friend I have is really nice to me.

J anuary 1st is my birthday.
A mong Us is sus like Joe Mama.
N o broccoli for me, so don't even try.

Jan Kolankowski (10)
St George's Catholic Primary School, Sudbury Hill

A Recipe To Create Me

To create me, you will need:
2 tablespoons of maths, art, humanities, and science.
500 grams of Domino's pizza, burritos, tacos, burgers, and apples.
300 grams of Roblox and Warzone.
Add a piece of skin of Kane and Pickford
Add fun from a random day.

First you need to stir maths, art, humanities, and science,
After you've done that, add 500 grams of Domino's pizza, burrito, tacos, burgers, and apples.
Secondly, 300 grams of Roblox and Warzone.
Second last is to add a piece of Kane and Pickford skin.
Lastly, add fun from random day.

Gabriel Plusa (9)
St George's Catholic Primary School, Sudbury Hill

Jazzy James

Yeah, my name is James
I'm not a number one
My friend Terry is
He's not hairy.

My favourite word is banana
Even though I despise them
My real name is Jem King
I ain't a bad king
I also like showers
But not in the towers.

My favourite teacher is Miss Coleman
She taught me in Year Four
I also like Mr Lewis
People say I am him.

I am from Ireland
It ain't a far land
My dad is from Donegal
It is a big hall
Be careful not to fall.

I like jam doughnuts.
Yeah, yeah, yeah.

James McLaughlin (9)
St George's Catholic Primary School, Sudbury Hill

This Is Me!

Hi! Stefania's my name!
I don't like summer, I love the rain.
My dad tells me, "Don't wear shorts"
I'm excellent at water sports.

My zodiac sign is Gemini.
I've always wanted to be able to fly.
I might be a little obsessed with Netflix.
I'm really good at doing mind tricks.

I've met a dancing pigeon!
I drool when I see ice cream in the kitchen.
Speedy is my tortoise, she is very fast.
If you mess with my friends, this day will
be your last!

This is me!

Stefania Bukala (9)
St George's Catholic Primary School, Sudbury Hill

This Is Me, Mateusz

T his is me
H is name starts with an M and ends with Z
I s really brave and never gives up
S marter than you think.

I s always ready for snacks
S porty and loves football.

M ore excited than a child
E nthusiastic at every moment.

M ateusz is his name
A nd he has lots of friends
T he boy also has a turtle
E nergetic every day
U nexpected of anything
S illier than a monkey
Z est of excitement.

Mateusz Skrzynski (10)
St George's Catholic Primary School, Sudbury Hill

The Funny Bunny

Yo, my name is Francis Osmani,
I found a funny bunny that was eating honey.
Turns out it was my missing bunny,
It was weird because it likes honey.
I put my bunny in the cage
And tried to find my art supplies while my mum was making pies.
All I found was some ties but I did not cry,
Instead, I rapidly ate my pie,
And I devoured it with my power.
I was a coward because I devoured.
I doodle while I eat noodles,
I play Minecraft the game with my big brain,
My mum drinks tea while I pee, this is me!

Francis Osmani (9)
St George's Catholic Primary School, Sudbury Hill

This Is Me - Magnificent Maya

Ingredients:
100g of hard-working attitude
A slice of ambition
A teaspoon of adventure
A sprinkle of history
A pinch of creativeness
A dash of my friend Lily
2 teaspoons of kindness and fun.

Method:
1 - Cream the slice of ambition with the sprinkle of history.
2 - Add in the teaspoon of adventure and the pinch of creativeness.
3 - Mix the dash of my friend Lily and the 2 teaspoons of kindness and fun.
4 - Finally, add in the 100g of hard-working attitude.

This is me!

Maya Turner (10)
St George's Catholic Primary School, Sudbury Hill

I Am Who I Am

It started when I bumped my head,
I became weird, brave, and chatty,
Was it for the best? I don't know,
But life is short, the world is wide,
I wanna use the time I have,
Reach for the place no one else has,
I'm my own hero, don't have to have anyone else,
I go down the path I lead,
I want to speak to everyone I can,
Answer the world's questions,
Be who I am,
Not being swapped for this girl,
I know you want me,
But I'll be who I am,
Because this is me!

Amy Lorenzato (10)
St George's Catholic Primary School, Sudbury Hill

This Is Me, Jayden

I am a lightning bolt in football boots
I am a superstar striker
I play the drums every Monday
Sometimes I say I'm silly.

My friends say I'm funny
But I think I'm chatty
I'm always kind
I'm always in a good mood.

I love Chelsea
They're the best football team in the world
And I love basketball too
Michael Jordan is my favourite.

I am strong.
Sometimes I am brave
And I am sporty
And I love to rhyme.

Jayden Phillips-Clarke (9)
St George's Catholic Primary School, Sudbury Hill

This Is Me, Adam!

My name is Adam,
I am sporty,
I like playing football,
In the pool.
It's also fine on the grass.

My favourite team is Liverpool,
One of the players had a fall.
My favourite player is Mo Salah.

My eye colour is blue,
It is very true.
My hair is as brown as a tree.
I am Polish,
But I'm also English.

When I am older, I want to be a footballer.
If that doesn't work,
I'll be a guitarist.

This is me!

Adam Senftleben (10)
St George's Catholic Primary School, Sudbury Hill

How To Make Me

You need:
Food in a box
17 litres of books
19 grams of best friends
1 litre of 'E'
2 grams of 'VA'
Done!

First, add 15 out of 17 litres of books,
Add the food in a box.
Stir and add the other 2 litres of books.
Get a fresh bowl of the 19 grams of best friends and put them in the mix.
Whisk the 1 litre of "E" and the two grams of "V.A." into the mix.
Bake for 55 minutes, and done!

This is me!

Eva Kedroe (10)
St George's Catholic Primary School, Sudbury Hill

The Secret Ingredient To Me

So you want to make me, huh?
Here, listen to these instructions very carefully.

First, you will need ten scales of a lightning dragon,
The fur of a dog, a frying pan with an egg (not cracked),
The gills of an axolotl, and a paint bucket.

Now, these are the main ingredients.
You need a potion of silliness and mischief, a lot of it.
Absolute mountains of sushi.
A potion of hanging out with the boy and tennis
And *voila*, it's done.

Tara Lama (9)
St George's Catholic Primary School, Sudbury Hill

Happy Hanna The Animal Lover

H appy I am in different ways
A nd I always have a friend beside me
N ever get bored
N ever get angry
A nd I am really funny.

W henever my friends are sad I can cheer them up
E ver so happy
G ood and kind, of course I am
R unning around with my little brother
Z igzag trying to catch my pets
Y es, I am adventurous
K ind and friendly - that is me!

Hanna Wegrzyk (9)
St George's Catholic Primary School, Sudbury Hill

Adrian Is My Name And You Would Like It

T he best person you can ever meet.
H ave many vacations at the beach but I can take the heat.
I am very sporty because I am fast as lightning with boots.
S easide is the best place to be.

I 'm really smart and also very friendly.
S ometimes I am fearless and take risks.

M e and you will have the best time ever,
E lite as Mo Salah (the football player).

This is me!

Adrian Rajkumar (9)
St George's Catholic Primary School, Sudbury Hill

This Is Me, Tyler!

T yler, that is my name
H appiness is all I need but also my family
I love football, my dream is to become a pro
S kills, I know all of them.

I love my family, especially my mummy
S mart, I am smart but especially maths.

M aths is my favourite subject, I'll answer any question you throw at me
E verybody knows I'm Irish, so I'll always be green and orange at heart.

Tyler Roche (9)
St George's Catholic Primary School, Sudbury Hill

This Is Me!

Generous and kind
A super-fast mind
Maths is my superpower
History makes me dumb.

I swim, I sprint
I am a very sporty kid
I love basketball and
I know I'm awesome.

I'm sweet, I'm sour
Depending on the hour.
I'm friendly, I'm funny
Depending on you!

I'm hard-working
Curious and passionate
And I will make you smile
So this is me!

Angel Vijeyechandren (9)
St George's Catholic Primary School, Sudbury Hill

My Daily Life

My name is Star I always
Have time to say "Ta!"
I love to eat sushi it makes
Me go all fruity. Animal Crossing
Always has me thinking what's next
To buy when I next go shopping!

My pet George is always here when
I get bored, Tara Lama is here
When I fall. Ms Magar is always there
When my work is hard and I feel scared
Micah and Josiah always care!

This is me!

Star Scarlett (10)
St George's Catholic Primary School, Sudbury Hill

This Is Me!

Yeah, yeah, yeah
I'm playing football
Yeah
I don't eat sweets, yeah
Playing with Calixo
And my other friends, yeah.

I don't like Man U but I like Chelsea.
I like basketball, playing with
Michatron X and his brother, yeah, RXP
Kyron likes playing 'It', yeah
He can 'It' everyone, but me
Because I'm too quick, yeah
This is me.

Aaron Lewis (10)
St George's Catholic Primary School, Sudbury Hill

This Is Me

- **C** reative and bubbly, that's me!
- **L** ove of art, I'm smart!
- **O** pposite of glum, that's for sure!
- **T** alkative, a lot of that, I'm a chatterbox.
- **H** ilarious and silly,
- **I** 'm a good actor, and I'm funny,
- **L** aughing all the time, making people laugh.
- **D** auntless and bold.
- **E** nergetic and sporty, that's me!

Clothilde Salord (10)
St George's Catholic Primary School, Sudbury Hill

This Is Me

This is me, I live with my family,
My family is the best.
People call me Alice, but my name is Alicja.
I am ten years old, I like games.
I play with my brother and puppy.
My favourite sport is basketball and swimming.
My favourite colour is purple.

My nationality is English and Polish.
I like doing arts and crafts.
But the thing that inspires me is nature.

Alicja Prystasz (10)
St George's Catholic Primary School, Sudbury Hill

My Pet

My pet is a mystery, can you guess it?
A creature living in the house.
It does not have wings, it cannot fly.
Black and white with a hint of brown.
It's eight months old!
And pretty naughty!
It's very cute, and it's a girl.
You can't guess it!
She is very playful, and pretty rough.
What is it?

¡bop ∀ :ɹǝmsu∀

Adriana Romanska (9)
St George's Catholic Primary School, Sudbury Hill

Cool Bull

Yo, my name is Tymon
I like my movies with a demon
I am always me
My sister hates bees
I always swim in seas
I climb on tall trees
I really like TVs
My mom drinks teas
I'm running from a disease
I do some doodles
My sister likes noodles
I like my game
I have a big brain
I really like my name
And this is me!

Tymon Jankowicz (9)
St George's Catholic Primary School, Sudbury Hill

George

G eorge is my name, my nickname is Big Chungus!
E ager to play football, I love Manchester City.
O utside is the best place for me to be.
R eally good at maths, I love multiplication.
G aming is my thing, Roblox is the best.
E njoyable is what most people call me!

C ats are the best!

George Coelho (10)
St George's Catholic Primary School, Sudbury Hill

Star Winger

I'm Freddie, I'm a mamma's boy.
My life is filled with so much joy,
My favourite sport is football,
But I'm very, very small.

I love Brazil.
My dad supports Liverpool; that makes me ill.
Arsenal are the best,
But don't tell, my dad is a pest,
and my life is always the best.

Freddie Thompson (9)
St George's Catholic Primary School, Sudbury Hill

This Is Me

T iny in size
H is name starts with an R and ends with a Y
I 'm good at sports and gaming
S o would you play against me?

I t's nice to be me
S marter than you think.

M y name is Riley
E veryone loves me.

And that was me!

Riley Walter Jordan (9)
St George's Catholic Primary School, Sudbury Hill

This Is Me Rap

Yeah
This is me
I'm full of glee
I don't like meat
It's not my treat.

I'm ten years old
And I was told
That I wasn't sold
Especially for gold.

I like football
I always score.

And yet again
This is me.
My name is
Arsenie.

Arsenie Boca (10)
St George's Catholic Primary School, Sudbury Hill

Julia Acrostic Poem

T his is me.
H ave fun dreams and silly ones.
I love my family.
S un is my favourite weather.

I have a fun teacher and very good friends.
S illy like a clown.

M e and my family are amazing.
E asy-going.

And that is me!

Julia Baran (9)
St George's Catholic Primary School, Sudbury Hill

A Recipe To Me!

You will need:
A tablespoon of laughter
500g of maths
A pinch of shyness
Five potatoes
10ml of gymnastics.

Stir a tablespoon of laughter with 10ml of gymnastics.
Add a pinch of shyness to the mix.
Add the potatoes one at a time.
500g of maths should finish it off.

Charlize Yu (10)
St George's Catholic Primary School, Sudbury Hill

This Is Me!

T he best person on Earth is me
H appy is my thing
I love to play Roblox
S eals are the best.

I like to do RE
S ometimes I play on the Nintendo Switch.

M cDonald's is tasty
E nd, my name is Lena!

Lena Kostuj (9)
St George's Catholic Primary School, Sudbury Hill

Dave The Dog

He barks at trees
He jumps on your knees
He knows when you're sad
He does not get mad
He loves treats
He does not sleep
He loves toys
He does not annoy
He does not like cats
That is that
I love my dog Dave
He is great.

Holly Masterson (9)
St George's Catholic Primary School, Sudbury Hill

This Is Me!

T his is me
H ave four dogs
I ce cream is my favourite
S easide is my favourite

I have three brothers
S wimming is my favourite

M y mum cooks the best food
E xcited for bed!

Olivia O'Leary (9)
St George's Catholic Primary School, Sudbury Hill

Ayden

A stands for adventurous, active person!
Y stands for yummy yolk!
D stands for your destructive desk!
E stands for epic, energetic Ayden!
N starts for your nutritious nose!

Ayden Bonsu (9)
St George's Catholic Primary School, Sudbury Hill

This Is Me

My name is Josh
I like football
I'm a star striker
In my shiny football boots.

My favourite food is chips
It's my favourite dish.
I don't like fish!

This is me!

Josh (10)
St George's Catholic Primary School, Sudbury Hill

This Is Me

A mazing player and a football fan.
N egotiate cards and items.
D umb and funny.
R ick-rolling people and hilarious jokes.
E lite pro-FIFA gamer and super adventurous.

Andre Khayrallah (10)
St George's Catholic Primary School, Sudbury Hill

This Is Me

Hi, my name is Kyron,
I like playing basketball.
I live with my family.
I am ten years old.
I wish I could go to Lapland because it's marvellous.
My favourite sport is swimming and football.

Kyron St Clair (10)
St George's Catholic Primary School, Sudbury Hill

Who Am I?
A kennings poem

Caregiver
Planet saver
TV presenter
Rubbish picker
Animal lover
Creature assister
Kind sir
Life changer
Scriptwriter
Stuff recycler
Planet fixer
Animal saver
Book lover
Nature filmer
Earth lover
Smart man
Polite presenter
Day guider
Tea sipper
Autobiography writer

Family carer
Inspiring leader
Charity donator
Life saver
People helper
Blue Peter
Ninety-two years.

Answer: David Attenborough.

Sarah Hyland (10)
St Mary's Catholic Primary School, Gillingham

Who Is It?

A kennings poem

Wonderful woman
Amazing activist
Accomplished attempter
Surprising speech
Lovely lady
Sweet speaker
Determined debater
Decision demander
Sensitive supporter
Youthful wonder
Independently inspirational
Quiet queen
Often opener
Important ideas
Key knowledge
Famous face
Shot at school
Such success
Wonderful work

Look at the poem so you can see
Who do you think it could really be?

Answer: Malala.

Victoria Irodalo (10)
St Mary's Catholic Primary School, Gillingham

Who Am I?
A kennings poem

Phone lover
Game player
Song singer
Great adviser
Lace tier
Child protector
Jacket-zipper
Tub opener
Epic listener
Door locker
Big yawner
Movie watcher
Toy fixer
Coffee consumer
Big shopper
Weather forecaster
Big hugger
Drink refiller
Homework helper
TV lover

Strong leader
Powerful teacher
Injury healer
Stylish dresser
Best lover
Story writer
Big shopper
The best friend.

Jacinta Barclay (9)
St Mary's Catholic Primary School, Gillingham

Who Am I?
A kennings poem

Gives laughter
Moderately famous
Long sleeper
TV watcher
Advice giver
Storyteller
Dog lover
Heroic guide
Shelter giver
Friendly heart
Spiky beard
Loving person
Smiling sunshine
Homework solver
Cappucino drinker
Lego builder
Family lover

My friend.
Who am I?

Answer: Dad.

Melody Chang (10)
St Mary's Catholic Primary School, Gillingham

Joke Teller
A kennings poem

Joke teller
Great gifter
First friend
Book-lover
Funny-writer
Laughing reader
Give-sweet
Sarcastic friend
Roller coaster lover
Sweet lover
Problem-solver
Wobbly tooth hater
Movie lover
Animal lover
Bright mind
Backflip lover
Nice gassy
Blow liker
Eyes like the sky

Who am I?

Ugochi Ikebudu (9)
St Mary's Catholic Primary School, Gillingham

Who Am I?

A kennings poem

Loving person
Moderately famous
Good comedian
Cat lover
Device watcher
Gives laughter
Favourite's yellow
Writes tons
Severely sarcastic
Greatly generous
Magnificent helper
Coffee drinker
Sunlight smiles
Enormous heart
First aider.
Who am I?

Answer: My uncle Bogdan Honciuc.

Ilinca Honciuc (10)
St Mary's Catholic Primary School, Gillingham

Who Am I?
A kennings poem

G-force experiencer
Kin misser
Famous teacher
Flight simulator
Confident communicator
Planetary mechanic
Problem solver
Tension builder
Brave adventurer
Intergalactic explorer
Space walker
Moon lander
Footstep printer
Who am I?

Answer: I am Neil Armstrong.

Andrei Spinache (9)
St Mary's Catholic Primary School, Gillingham

Who Am I?

A kennings poem

Brilliant helper
Joke teller
Super swimmer
Running racer
Lego lover
Extraordinary hider
Book bringer
Jumping jester
Music maker
Loud laughter
Science studied
Chain reaction
Game winner
Technic teacher
Epic informer
Grateful giver
My friend.

Louis Dambreville-Harker (9)
St Mary's Catholic Primary School, Gillingham

Guess Who?
A kennings poem

Charity donator
Exceptional reliever
Phenomenal motivator
Extreme worker
Money aider
Tactical assister
Creative player
Frequent respecter
Confident devisor
Challenge conqueror
Challenge assister
Sadness preventer.

Answer: LaMelo Ball.

Samuel Uzoegbu (10)
St Mary's Catholic Primary School, Gillingham

Who Am I?

A kennings poem

School bestie
Skipping saviour
Amazing helper
Fantastic chatterer
Wild supporter
Inspirational beauty
Sweet singer
Pretty helper
Super star!
Kind smart
Sweeter than sugar
Brightest star
Boldest personality
Strong Skye
We're BFFs forever.

Chloe Chapman (10)
St Mary's Catholic Primary School, Gillingham

Who Am I?

A kennings poem

Life saver
Book lover
Funny reader
Challenge setter
Smart writer
Cat adorer
Education guider
Family carer
Team leader
Polite manner
Animal helper
Charity donator
Jesus praiser.
Guess who?

Answer: She's Miss Johnson.

Osaremen Atoe (10)
St Mary's Catholic Primary School, Gillingham

Who Am I?
A kennings poem

Fun player.
Good actor.
Pleasant maker.
Gorgeous blazer.
Funny walker.
Sleep destroyer.
Life liver.
Okay cooker.
Friend giver.
Person helper.
TikTok watcher.
Nice lighter.
Jealous destroyer.
Fun provider.
Pretty blazer.
Good friend.

Sophia Goulette (9)
St Mary's Catholic Primary School, Gillingham

Guess Who?
A kennings poem

Backboard destroyer
Colossal dunker
Trainer assister
Mindful baller
Amicable resister
Great lover
Personal guider
Company builder
Non-fictioner
Child
Immense challenger
Challenge dominater.

Answer: Shaquille O'Neal.

Isaiah Nzau (10)
St Mary's Catholic Primary School, Gillingham

Who Am I?

A kennings poem

Immense hugger
Dog lover
Advice giver
Kind guider
Fact knower
Passionate reader
Mess hater
Great leader
Influential helper
Generous protector
Cake baker
Problem preventer
Caring supporter.

Answer: My best friend!

Annie-Rose Cornelius (9)
St Mary's Catholic Primary School, Gillingham

Blue Mystery

A kennings poem

Flash dasher
Blue blur
Eggman stopper
Speedy power
Accident maker
Building breaker
Life changer
Owl mother
Tremendous saver
Sleep hater
Living joker
Apartment bedroom
Flash lover
Enemy Eggman
Ring welder
Speed power.

Jaiden Pitan (10)
St Mary's Catholic Primary School, Gillingham

Who Am I?
A kennings poem

Beautiful braids
Tall legs
Neat handwriter
Frizzy curls
Party animal
Reliable friend
Endless love
Infinity kindness
Loving forgiving
Incredible talented
Big brains
Nigerian girl
Roblox player
TikTok lover
Funny friend.

Sariyah Davis (10)
St Mary's Catholic Primary School, Gillingham

Who Am I?

A kennings poem

Always supportive
Addictive TT
Loves games
Really helpful
Super crazy
Kinda lazy
Extremely pretty
Loves food
Sometimes shy
A bit annoying
Together forever
Smile maker
Gives happiness
McDonald's lover
My inspiration.

Connie Brosnan (10)
St Mary's Catholic Primary School, Gillingham

Who Am I?

A kennings poem

Brand owner
Stranger Things
American actress
Famous celebrity
Role model
Friendly person
Short hair
Wrist tattoo
Nose bleed
Has telekinesis
Glasses wearer
Disney lover
Inspiration superstar
Dog person
Smart girl.

Tabitha Brown (10)
St Mary's Catholic Primary School, Gillingham

Who Am I?
A kennings poem

Devious dad
Never noisy
Superb shouter
Lively lad
Loves schnauzers
Loathes waiting
Funny artist
Funny laughter
Excellent actor
Silly joker
Loves gaming
Sometimes bad
Swimming expert
Jubilant dad
Stamp spotter.

Jakub Przybyla (9)
St Mary's Catholic Primary School, Gillingham

Who Am I?

A kennings poem

Pink lover
Great singer
Brilliant drawer
Amazing giver
Best writer
Great reader
Storyteller
Story writer
Always loving
Always kind
Neat writer
Best cowerer
Rainbow lover.

Answer: My cousins.

Grace Rajput (9)
St Mary's Catholic Primary School, Gillingham

Guess Who?
A kennings poem

Goal scorer
Foot guider
Loves football
High booter
Time keeper
Energy guzzler
Kind person
Block guider
Challenge settler
Ball giver
From Portugal
Thirty-six years.
Who am I?

Cristiano Ronaldo.

Finley Elnaugh (9)
St Mary's Catholic Primary School, Gillingham

Guess Who?
A kennings poem

Comedy writer
Idea giver
Funny reader
Great author
Generous guider
Kind explorer
Helpful hero
Serious autographer
Publisher signer
Publisher signer.
Who is it?

Answer: It is Jeff Kinney.

Ethan Redshaw (9)
St Mary's Catholic Primary School, Gillingham

My Friend Sunny

A kennings poem

My BFF
Amazing friend
Kind-hearted
Zealous personality
Happiness giver
Super jubilant
Funny king
Fantastic teammate
First friend
Sensational helper
Happy bringer
God destroyer
Who am I?

Alexander Hales (10)
St Mary's Catholic Primary School, Gillingham

Who Am I?

A kennings poem

Education lover
Maths educator
Wire fixer
Screw turner
Loud yawner
Occasional sleeper
Old fellow
Love giver
Time spender
Clever teacher
Newspaper reader.

Answer: My grandad.

Chidubem Uche (9)
St Mary's Catholic Primary School, Gillingham

Who Am I?
A kennings poem

Helpful healer
Light guider
Storyteller
Miracle doer
World maker
Fortune teller
Sin cleanser
Friend maker
Best prayer
Person maker
World's ruler
World's lighter
Our saviour.

Greg Ehigie (9)
St Mary's Catholic Primary School, Gillingham

Who Am I?
A kennings poem

Work helper
Helps me
Dinner cooker
He's kind
Good helper
Loves me
Bike helper
Really amazing
Forgives me
Cooking teacher
Grandma helper
No liar
Church preacher.

Kaima Eneh (10)
St Mary's Catholic Primary School, Gillingham

What Am I?
A kennings poem

House helper
Handsome chap
Hard worker
Clothes provider
Forgiving guy
Utensil washer
Laundry lover
Careful cooker
Great person
Honest human
Inspirational peep
What am I?

Chigozie Ejiofor (10)
St Mary's Catholic Primary School, Gillingham

Who Am I?
A kennings poem

Earth lover
Animal lover
A recycler
Planet carer
Environment protector
Earth cleaner
Great educator
Exciting smile
Nature rescuer.

Answer: David Attenborough.

Rhisiart Mabale (10)
St Mary's Catholic Primary School, Gillingham

A Great Inspiration
A kennings poem

Who am I?
India's feeder
Starvation destroyer
Selfless nourisher
Multilingual speaker
Generous giver
Famine curer
Poverty banisher
Hard worker
A phenomenal inspiration.

Gargi Raote (9)
St Mary's Catholic Primary School, Gillingham

Who Is This?
A kennings poem

Book lover
Children aider
People laughter
Book writer
Storyteller
Fiction envisioner
Big donator
Life lover
Amusing comedian

Answer: David Baddiel.

Kiril Rumiancev (10)
St Mary's Catholic Primary School, Gillingham

Who Am I?
A kennings poem

Big hugger
Homework helper
Tea drinker
Storyteller
Passionate reader
Funny helper
Magnanimous leader
Generous protector
Influential reader
Loving supporter.
Who am I?

Aoife Lidsey (9)
St Mary's Catholic Primary School, Gillingham

Who Am I?

A kennings poem

Football player
Game shatterer
Altruistic donater
Healthy muncher
Skilled sportsman
Money maker
Famous face
Goal getter
Family container
Supercar owner
Plane keeper.

Ryan Faradi (10)
St Mary's Catholic Primary School, Gillingham

Who Am I?
A kennings poem

Smart friend
Loud gamer
Football rescuer
Children helper
Animal lover
Goal scorer
Millionaire man
Hair maker
Funny comedian.

Answer: David Beckham.

Semilore Oluwatise (10)
St Mary's Catholic Primary School, Gillingham

Who Am I?
A kennings poem

Roblox player
Football admirer
Netball hater
Jewellery hater
Journey lover
Lazy laughter
Enormous enjoyer
Inspiration forever
Permanently family...
My cousin.

Anthony Hilla (9)
St Mary's Catholic Primary School, Gillingham

What Am I?
A kennings poem

Great inspiration
House cleaner
House cooker
Money provider
Family supporter
Dish cleaner
Fantastic discusser
Dreadful shouter
Laundry washer
Funny parents.

Janica Barcelona (10)
St Mary's Catholic Primary School, Gillingham

Who Am I?
A kennings poem

Novel scribbler
Game developer
Generous grinner
Friendly donator
Idea granter
Smiling assister
Writing guider
Supporting repairer
Happy fixer
Big brainiac.

Oliver Perez (9)
St Mary's Catholic Primary School, Gillingham

Who Am I?

A kennings poem

Lifegiver
Kind lover
Friendly helper
Hard worker
Best friend
Sarcastic laughter
Fantasy reader
Best cleaner
Bath sleeper
Social guidance
Maths hater.

Kaden Banner (9)
St Mary's Catholic Primary School, Gillingham

Who Am I?
A kennings poem

Really friendly
Ball hogger
Really cool
Hard-working
Epic listener
Super fast
Amazing right winger
Murderous right winger
Ball protector
Brave footballer.

Ollie Blee (9)
St Mary's Catholic Primary School, Gillingham

Who Am I?
A kennings poem

Movie actor
Amazing suits
Saves people
Web flyer
Love spiders
Amazing powers
Wall climber
Web slinger
In love
Quick thinker
Good fighter
Is young.

Sammy Major (10)
St Mary's Catholic Primary School, Gillingham

Who Am I?

A kennings poem

Computer typer
Joke teller
Guides me
Good writer
Funny friend
Caring lady
Loving lady
Giving lady.

Answer: It's my mum.

Jack Raymond Clark (9)
St Mary's Catholic Primary School, Gillingham

Who Am I?
A kennings poem

School hater
Book reader
Animal lover
Roblox player
Joke maker
Great singer
Huge helper
Glasses wearer
Disney lover
Inspiring friend.

Beatrice Lapthorn (9)
St Mary's Catholic Primary School, Gillingham

Who Is He?

A kennings poem

Helping hand
Builder man
Independent man
Elderly known
Family man
Non-stop worker
Story teller
Super star
Jubilant man
Joyful adult.

Emmanuel David-Cole (10)
St Mary's Catholic Primary School, Gillingham

Who Am I?
A kennings poem

Car programmer
Game player
Fun provider
Dice roller
Maths challenger
Joke creator
Love giver
Generous helper
Great reader.
Who am I?

Zak Dempsay (10)
St Mary's Catholic Primary School, Gillingham

Samuel L Jackson

A kennings poem

Movie maker
Amazing actor
Perfect performer
Film producer
Well-known star
Succeeding accomplisher
TV entertainer
Award winner
My hero.

Sunny Ee (10)
St Mary's Catholic Primary School, Gillingham

Who Am I?
A kennings poem

Hard worker
Great carer
Fantastic helper
Incredible lover
Awesome listener
Nice motivator
Superb talker
Very talented
Wise choices.

Victor Emeakaroha (10)
St Mary's Catholic Primary School, Gillingham

Who Is It?

A kennings poem

Lorry driver
Football trainer
My friend
Joke teller
Tie whisper
Famous boss
Undoable doer

Who is it?

(My dad.)

Riley Peacock (9)
St Mary's Catholic Primary School, Gillingham

Who Am I?
A kennings poem

Amazing listener
Generous lover
Gentle healer
Loving sharer
Helpful giver
Lifesaver
Wisdom teacher
Storyteller
Love minder.

Mary-Lee Kempster (10)
St Mary's Catholic Primary School, Gillingham

Who Is She?
A kennings poem

My besider
Fantastic helper
House allower
Helpful accompanier
Amazing invader
YouTube TikToker
Clever, quieter
Ten years old.

Seren Roberts (10)
St Mary's Catholic Primary School, Gillingham

Who Am I?
A kennings poem

Goal scorer
Head kicker
Goal saver
Goalkeeper
Encouraging
Energy-dazzler
Miracle soccer
Bicycle kick
Miracle header.

Adams Ojo (10)
St Mary's Catholic Primary School, Gillingham

Who Am I?
A kennings poem

Excellent scorer
Class passer
Amazing dribbler
Amazing player
Identical teammate
Smart gamer
Super saver
Skilful shooter.

Thomas Rose (9)
St Mary's Catholic Primary School, Gillingham

Who Am I?
A kennings poem

Exceptionally smart
Assists me
Tremendously fast
Super fit
Sometimes whispers
Inspires me
BFFs forever
Amazingly fast.

Michael Farrell (9)
St Mary's Catholic Primary School, Gillingham

Who Am I?

A kennings poem

Child raiser
Successful driver
Hard worker
Fantastic cook
Love giver
Food hunter
Supporting lover.

Aaron Cuevas (10)
St Mary's Catholic Primary School, Gillingham

Who Am I?
A kennings poem

Fish lover
Bed stayer
Bird watcher
Bedroom invader
Leg scratcher
Mouse catcher
Perfect purrer.

Tyler Harwood (10)
St Mary's Catholic Primary School, Gillingham

Who Am I?
A kennings poem

First man
Moon stepper
Space lover
Brave adventurer
Smart trainer
Team maker
Space walker.

Jack Fordham (9)
St Mary's Catholic Primary School, Gillingham

Who Am I?
A kennings poem

People assister
Advice passer
People supporter
Kindness passer
Huge laugher
Information giver.

Danielis Sirvinskas (9)
St Mary's Catholic Primary School, Gillingham

Guess Me!
A kennings poem

Friendly guider
Advice giver
Student inspirer
Giver of help.

Answer: My coach!

Albert Stanley (9)
St Mary's Catholic Primary School, Gillingham

The Greatest Me!

This is how you make me (don't forget to bake me!).
First, you have to pour in creativity and fill it to the top,
Keep on going, don't stop!
Then pour in every drop of love,
Because love is what makes me graceful like a dove.
Now stir in all of that generosity,
Because it's an extremely positive part of me.
Next, fill it up with family love,
Because it's what I'm thinking of.
After you have done so, pour in enthusiasm,
Which is stronger than dynamite or super-plasm.
Finally, you are done,
And all of those ingredients will make your cake number one!

Sharon Akeju (10)
St Vincent's RC Primary School, Dagenham

Me

Hey, my name is Saphy
And I would really like a bunny
My friends think I'm funny
When I am older I would like to be a lawyer
And I'm quite an enjoyer
I'm a friend to all
Willing to help all those who call
I have respect for my teachers
But have no time for deceivers and cheaters
Saphy is strong, honest, and respectful
My mum always calls me 'princess', and 'beautiful'
I never get myself into trouble
Maths is always a puzzle
I always have muscle when it comes to dancing
And thank you for reading Saphy's life.

Saphron Serrant (10)
St Vincent's RC Primary School, Dagenham

The Time Has Come

The time has come,
The period of advent,
I go to reconciliation,
So I can repent.

The time has come,
The period of Christmas,
I eat some food,
That is very delicious.

The time has come,
It's New Year's Eve,
I stayed up till midnight,
With my cousin Marie.

The time has come,
It's the New Year,
There are fireworks,
And a great sense of cheer.

The time has come,
I am finally growing,
I'm learning new things,
Though my flaws are still showing.

Philippa Kanneh (11)
St Vincent's RC Primary School, Dagenham

My Mixed Emotions

I could be filled with love, nice and caring,
Or I could be full of anger.
So mad and daring, but there are ways to fix that,
Hanging with friends, the fun would never end.
Or doing the things I love most, like eating toast,
I like doing PE, though sometimes it's not easy.
Watching movies is my number one best,
It helps me take out all my stress.
Though when I'm sad, I listen to music.
It's a great way to help me through it.
Now you know I'm all about my commotions,
And I call them my mixed emotions.

Michaela Kondjo (10)
St Vincent's RC Primary School, Dagenham

Art

Creativity, such a wonderful thing,
And you don't need to have skills to
make something,
You can sculpt, paint, colour, and draw,
The choices are endless so you don't have
to be sure.
You can do it for fun or to heal your boredness,
And you can do absolutely anything,
Art is such madness, and if you like to draw things
That are a little bit weird,
You'll laugh like a hyena.
Art is for everyone around the world,
So go on, pick up a pencil, and give it a whirl.

Marie-Lou Yenga (11)
St Vincent's RC Primary School, Dagenham

Me And Me Only

Growing up wasn't easy,
Showing everyone my personality,
My journey was a little bit rough,
Taking everything in could be tough.

So many people wanted me to change,
While I wanted to stay the same.
When my loved ones were proud,
I felt on top of the clouds.

When I went to school,
I thought it was cruel,
I came in with pride,
And came out with a sigh.

And that's the story of me,
And me only,
(Also known as my life)!

Owen Orhue (11)
St Vincent's RC Primary School, Dagenham

Wave Of Fear

Fear is scary,
A lot of the time it varies,
Whether or not it controls you,
Or if it surrounds your soul.
Fear is everything we think about,
It is there when we rest
Sometimes it makes you stressed,
It is where when we eat,
It can raise your heartbeat,
Fear can be controlled,
It can be controlled with love,
But sometimes it needs a bit of a shove.
It's okay, though, fear can be stopped,
And can be swapped,
Swapped with love.

Gabriella Mazzon (11)
St Vincent's RC Primary School, Dagenham

The Magic Pencil

I take my pencil,
And I take my pen,
I draw very carefully,
I draw very zen.
My imagination runs through,
The magic pencil I hold.
I scribble pictures on paper,
And I whisper, "Behold!"
"A work of art!"
"A true masterpiece!"
"A gem I could treasure."
"Piece by piece!"
I look at the pencil, bright and bold,
A true mystery,
That, on paper, begins to unfold...

Sophie Perdoch (10)
St Vincent's RC Primary School, Dagenham

Training To Be The Best

I am the best player in the world
I love playing the beautiful game.
I have dreams like everyone else
But sometimes I need to take in the pain.

Sport brings me happiness
But sometimes brings me sadness.
So I need to take every chance
And can never say, "I can't."

My parents are on my side
As luck's hard to provide.

I go to school thinking about sport,
And that's only on my mind.

Eghosa Ekhosuehi (11)
St Vincent's RC Primary School, Dagenham

My World

I make mistakes like all people, but my mistakes are most clumsy.
I try my best every day, seems like I can't make a difference,
At least that's what I thought.
I've gained a loud mouth to speak to people,
Gaining friends along the way.
I'm happy and filled with excitement.
I don't ever feel happiness but that is what makes me.
My emotions feel like a roller coaster but that is what makes me.

Rich Kodua (10)
St Vincent's RC Primary School, Dagenham

Describe Your Personality

P eople person is really my thing
E nergetic around familiar faces
R arely talk around unfamiliar faces
S hy is a word often used to describe me
O n time
N ever being late for anything
A lways there for you
L oyal and will forever trust you
I will always try to get the best out of you
T rustworthy and loving
Y ou will always be known by me.

Frederica Sackey (10)
St Vincent's RC Primary School, Dagenham

It's All About Me

I am not for everyone.
I know who I am and what I will be.
I am like a jaguar: fast, independent,
But can be rather silent at times.
I bring love and strength where I go.

I am not for everyone.
I am not perfect,
But I still try to improve and reach my potential.
And if I don't fit in with a person or group, that's okay with me.
Because that's how life is meant to be.

Nathaniel Oluwasokale (11)
St Vincent's RC Primary School, Dagenham

Justice

J ust show kindness, it is right,
U nderestimating isn't okay, even when it's slight,
S o don't expect to be saved, be a saviour,
T he future you get depends on your behaviour,
I t is important when you learn,
'C ause that's when life takes a turn,
E very moment, every minute.

Justice should be served!

Michelle Nyarko (10)
St Vincent's RC Primary School, Dagenham

Merlin

My name is Merlin,
And I live in Berlin.
I would really like a pony,
But it might be naughty.
Isabella is my friend,
She is really nice,
Just don't get on her bad side.
My dad is a lawyer,
My mum's a nurse,
She can go crazy if,
I get sick.
My dad is really boring,
He's a good friend to me.
I love Berlin,
I love everyone.

Olatoye Oguntoye (10)
St Vincent's RC Primary School, Dagenham

Sports Are Fun!

I like sports, a lot of sports, and I play them safely and well!
I like competitive sports where I can help out my team,
And it's not about winning, it's that we enjoy doing it,
And have fun while trying to do so.
Try your best, believe in you and your squad,
If you give someone courage,
They'll give courage to you when needed.

Lloyd Ackerson (11)
St Vincent's RC Primary School, Dagenham

2022 Summer For Cats

Gentle eyes that see too much,
Claws that have a deafening touch,
Purrs to say, "Tell us well,"
Or you won't be well.
Quiet moments touched with pride,
Imaginary comes to my side,
So small they can be,
Like my cup of tea,
They can bite,
They can hiss,
But they will never know our love for them!

Paulina Geldon (10)
St Vincent's RC Primary School, Dagenham

New Horizons

Not saying life's perfect, obviously not!
But enjoy and love what I've got.
Last year wasn't my time to shine,
But this time, it's my turn in line!

The stars are aligned perfectly,
And time seems to work with me!
What I am saying is that this is my time.
This new horizon will finally be mine!

Peyton Cryillia Marina Shillingford (11)
St Vincent's RC Primary School, Dagenham

A Day At The Tracks

R oaring engines around the track
A collision on corner three
C ars crazily zooming past
E very vehicle has a number plastered on it
C haos around each bend
A round the home straight, the chequered flag flies
R ight at the last minute, the underdog steals the win.

Jimmy Wilkins (10)
St Vincent's RC Primary School, Dagenham

Sadness Sickness

Sadness is a creature who lives in the deepest, darkest tunnels of your soul.
His skin is blue and his eyes are purple.
He makes you sniffle, cry, and feel blue.
What you have to do is ignore him, then he will tease someone else.
He might come back another day as he is not afraid.

Loraly Peta (10)
St Vincent's RC Primary School, Dagenham

What Makes Me

E xcellent behaviour anywhere,
T ries to cheer people up if they're sad,
H elpful and listens to instructions,
A lways tries their hardest,
N ever gives up and keeps on persevering.

This is me!

Ethan Doogan (10)
St Vincent's RC Primary School, Dagenham

My Colombian Flag

My Colombian flag has three colours, yellow, blue, and red.
Yellow represents our golden sunshine.
Blue represents our beautiful oceans and our blue skies.
Red represents the red roses that grow all over our country.

Kristian Marquez Ospina (11)
St Vincent's RC Primary School, Dagenham

Summer Is About To Start Soon

S andcastles I make on the beach
U mbrellas behind you so you don't burn
M eet people at the beach
M ake slushies all day
E at ice cream to cool down
R un through the sprinklers.

Mia Vaskeviciute (11)
St Vincent's RC Primary School, Dagenham

Me And My Furby Boom

Once there was a boy named Michael.
His dad had bought a gift for him.
Michael opened his gift.
It was a Furby Boom.
"Hello Furby Boom," said Michael.
Furby Boom liked Michael.
Michael liked Furby Boom.

Michael Oluyemi (10)
St Vincent's RC Primary School, Dagenham

YOUNG WRITERS INFORMATION

We hope you have enjoyed reading this book – and that you will continue to in the coming years.

If you're the parent or family member of an enthusiastic poet or story writer, do visit our website **www.youngwriters.co.uk/subscribe** and sign up to receive news, competitions, writing challenges and tips, activities and much, much more! There's lots to keep budding writers motivated!

If you would like to order further copies of this book, or any of our other titles, then please give us a call or order via your online account.

Young Writers
Remus House
Coltsfoot Drive
Peterborough
PE2 9BF
(01733) 890066
info@youngwriters.co.uk

Join in the conversation!
Tips, news, giveaways and much more!

YoungWritersUK **YoungWritersCW** **youngwriterscw**